Breaking

The

Silence

Writing by Asian Women

This book wasn't written by any one or two people. It is the product of a whole range of help and support from very many people, mainly from within our Asian community. The most important thanks goes to the women whose writing is published here. Women who we cannot Name, but who we thank for their bravery.

We would like also to thank Miss Farahna, Amarjit Kaur, Mrs. C. Palmer and Maya Sen for their work in translating the writing; Ann Goode and Maureen O'Hagen for their work in typing; Miss Palmer of Montem School for allowing us to take photographs in her class and Anima Bannarjee for agreeing to be photographed; Helen, Liz, Carol, Dee, Nina and everyone else at Dalston Children's Centre.

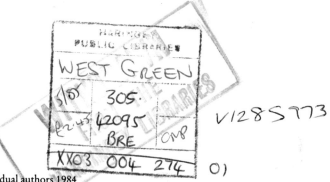
© Individual authors 1984
Published by Centerprise Trust Ltd, 136 Kingsland High St.
London E8 in association with Dalston Childrens Centre.
Typeset and printed by Lithosphere Printing Co-operative
203 Pentonville Rd., London N1

Centerprise Trust is grateful for financial assistance from
the Inner London Education Authority, Hackney Borough Council,
the Greater London Arts Association and the Greater London
Council.
ISBN 0 903738 64 3

PREFACE

Manju and Anna's approach to us about publishing Breaking the Silence represents a new way of working for us. Rather than setting up the project ourselves, or deciding to work towards the publication of an individual's writing, we were presented with a fairly advanced project. Our initial role was to advise on the practical side of publishing and, through co—publication with Dalston Children's Centre, distribute the book. As time went by, we became more involved with co—ordinating and editorial work than any of us had at first envisaged. The process of working through a new, and sometimes difficult, relation to publishing: where we were more of a resource to be drawn on than directors of the project; will stand us in good stead for future collaborations.

We hope this book will be read and used in a variety of ways. In Mother Tongue Language classes; in schools to stimulate discussion with Asian and non—Asian groups of children and teenagers; by Asian parents as a way of understanding their daughters and by those daughters as a way of understanding their parents. We believe, too, that making visible some experiences of the lives of women often hidden within their own, and our dominant white, culture is a valuable project of interest to all those concerned with the contemporary position of women. We know Asian women and girls who have broken through some of the barriers and silences that are the concern of this book, but their experience is not central here. That does not mean that we don't respect or acknowledge the Asian women organising politically within the feminist movement, the ones who have come out as lesbians or the ones at the centre of anti—racist and immigration struggles. We see their lives as linked with those represented here but have chosen to prioritise the more often silenced women who begin to speak to you through these pages.

Centerprise Publishing Project
August 1984

Contents

INTRODUCTION

I think it was a great adventure for me when I was asked to do the Asian Women's book project by Dalston Children's Centre where I work. From my own life and talking to many Asian women, young and old, I realise there is a cry, conflict, pressure and pride inside me. I find it very difficult to expose my feeling, I think because of my upbringing and the restriction I had to have. Now it is just a way of life—carry on and pretend to live happily for ever, only to think of the family, ignoring "me", the my ownself. And I know many other Asian women share that experience as well.

I knew it won't be an easy task. Also, if I don't write how I have got the writings the book will not be complete. First we did 200 leaflets explaining the idea that group of Asian women will come to Dalston Children's Centre, exchange their ideas and write. Anna will do photography with the group too. I distributed the leaflet among the girls and women I knew, also those I came across in the street and market. It was publicised in Outwrite and our newsletter and the leaflet distributed to Community Centres and Groups. Because of lack of response I became very frustrated. Anna and me started to meet every Thursday. It is her who kept me going till today for Asian women book project.

At the end, the writing I have got through my personal approach. The girls and women who talked to me were not prepared to join a group. They were frightened of offending their families. Some of them I meet at bus stops, park, market etc. During that period I experienced that women are fighting to express their true feelings living in two cultures, though this book is not the book we hoped for. Unfortunately in this book we could not include the Asian women who are involved in the Feminist movement, who are leading their own lives rather than conventional lifestyle. The cause is when I approach them either they are too busy, lack of time, also some of them are not willing, could be pressure of their own lives. There are Asian women who are Doctors, Lawyers, Teachers—and politically fighting for their skin, rights and language in this racist society. They do make sure their voices heard. It is not true that Asian women spend their lives only in a kitchen. So in a way quite important other women must be heard and recognised. Those who are not politically active, perhaps they can't afford to be?

I did assure them no names will be published. The women who are under pressure it was very difficult to meet them. Once I visited a house, woman made sure father would be out. Mother don't speak English—I don't speak her language. She asked me through her daughter that her daughter not married off yet—hope I will remember I did assure her no harm comes to her daughter if she writes. The times I went to her house I was given wonderful food, when I was coming back I was given food for my family. Now I have got around 25 writings—but it has taken for me many days of talking, visits to mothers and lots of phone calls to the women and their families. During that time my friends at Centre, collective, were always helpful whenever I needed time off. In this connection, I must mention my friend and aunt, Maya Sen (Krishna's mother). Her encouragement and help made this book possible as well.

There are some mothers who really wanted to come out and tell people about their life, but they are under pressure. I meet some young women who are very bitter, too frighten to talk and write. So my feeling about the writing is, is not the whole truth what I expected. Idea of the book is to present the feelings of Asian women of their lives, how they are coping within the two worlds. If I can say, some of the women I know, outside they be Doctors, Teachers but as soon as they are inside home, back to nursing an old mother—in—law, or taking care of kitchen which is left for her to mind as she is woman. Still it is a step and courageous for these women to write which will encourage other Asian women to write. From my visit to Local School's Asian Girls group, I can realise there is a great urge among second and third generation of young women to rebel against the tradition up to a certain extent. Most of them don't want to reject their traditional culture—just want some understanding and support from their parents. Older generation's expectation and exploitation in many cases too much. One girl is born here, brought up in this racist society—in most cases parents expect her like a girl born in Karachi or Bombay—instead of an apple, expecting a Mango. It will be easier for young Asian women to cope with their everyday life if they have this understanding. But some Asian women told me they don't feel different. I felt, perhaps, few occasions I offended them identifying them as Asian women. That is something they want badly to forget. Many girls complain that parents let the brothers stay out late etc. From my experience I know many cases parents had to give in on their son's demands rather than losing their son. To keep the family together it is important for an Asian family.

After getting the writings we felt thrown into another problem. Publishing the book and how to go about it. We approach Centerprise, they agreed to do the book. Maggie and Rebecca taught us lot, now Anna and me feel without their help this book wouldn't be possible at all. Working with them matter of fact encouraging me to do another book. This support is so strong and valuable— also making me feel I can write a book even!

As an Asian woman I am in this country last 17 years. One thing I noticed, we are taken for granted: nice, soft and sari clad, Timid little things, by white society. It is not going to be same with next generation. They will question this expectation of them and want a clear answer. As a whole, women all over the world under the pressure end up with raw deal. To fight that black sisters need help from their white sisters—sisterhood is the weapon for fight back.

Manju

This introduction is also available in Bengali, Gujeratti, Hindi, Punjabi, Urdu. If you would like to receive a copy please send 50p, stating which language required, and a S.A.E. to the publishers.

ABOUT THE PHOTOGRAPHS

I became involved with this project through my work running a women's photography workshop at the Dalston Children's Centre. When Manju and I first talked about working on a book we hoped that the women and girls who did the writing would take the photographs themselves using the facilities at the centre. This was not possible as they were not able to come to the centre and it was important not to identify them for the reasons Manju has explained in her introduction. To get around this problem, and also in order to try to avoid 'stereotypes', I based most of the photographs around one day in the life of Manju and her daughter Shaoli. Obviously each day is unique to each person and only reveals some aspect of their lives. Working on this project has been very rewarding and stimulating for me. I could not have done it without Manju's friendship and support and the hospitality shown to me by the Asian community.

Anna

MY MOTHER DIDN'T LIKE IT

I have been living in England since I was 6 years old, having come over with my family from Kenya. We moved straight to London where some of my relatives were already living. My childhood was pretty 'normal'. I have a sister who is 6 years older, and my two brothers were born after we arrived in England. However, this normal, average childhood, was drastically altered due to the sudden death of my father, who died when I was just 11. From that day on, I cannot claim to have had a normal Punjabi Sikh upbringing, or a normal childhood.

School was a comprehensive mixed school. I had many English and West Indian friends. I started to socialise with them at an early age (15). I wanted to go to school discos etc. My mother didn't like it but I didn't really respect her. I never thought about what her life was like or the difficulties she was always experiencing being a widow with 4 difficult to manage and control offsprings.

I went through stages of wishing I was white so I could have more freedom to socialise with my friends, being Asian seemed to me somehow seen as undesirable. The clothes they wear, the food is seen as being smelly and horrible, the 'funny' language all made me wish I was something else. However, this feeling was short lived. As I went through my teens, I learned more about my family what life was like in Kenya. I took more of an interest in the food and language and no longer felt embarassed to be different from my white peers. I asked myself what was so great about wanting to be white. Nothing was my conclusion I was grateful for having come from such a large family who are suportive, loving and caring. My aunts and uncles treat me and my brothers and sisters as their own. I have so many cousins that I get on very well with and go out with them regularly. This pleases our mothers very much.

Even though I now live away from home, I still go home almost every weekend to see my mother. I keep close contact with my cousins too. I want to show my mother that she has nothing to feel ashamed about because I live away from home. She knows why I moved. It was impossible to study at home because of my noisy brothers and also the constant visits from relatives were disruptive to my studying. A few of my cousins also lived away whilst they were studying for their degrees. So it wasn't difficult for me. The fact that I was going to Poly was the only reason why I was allowed to live away.

Unfortunately for my mother, I have now lived away from home for 3 years and could never live at home again. I have come to enjoy the freedom and independence and responsibilities of adulthood which I am not given when I am at my mother's. She has the ability of reducing me to an inconfident child. I become irritable very quickly and because of this we argue a great deal. She hates my lifestyle and the fact that I am independent. Asian parents like their children to be dependent on them until the day they marry, only then do the parents feel happy to let their child move away from home whatever their age.

The question of marriage always creates a great rift between myself and my mother. However, as yet the pressure of marriage is not upon me but upon my elder sister who is 27 and still single. I don't think either of us will have an arranged marriage because we have integrated and developed too much of the western way of thinking. I think this is very sad and unfortunate. I don't like to be 'caught' between two completely opposite ways of thinking. I do know that I will probably either not marry at all, or marry someone of my choice be it Asian, West Indian, English, whatever, and so will have to face the consequences of probably losing my family. Because I love them so much I don't want things to end up like that so I have no idea what I will do.

My concerns at the moment are not about the great turmoil and disaster marriage will cause, but about my studies and career. I cannot and will not let my family interfere in these matters.

DILJEET

ਮੇਰੀ ਮਾਂ ਨੂੰ ਵਿਚਰਣ ਪਸੰਦ ਨਹੀਂ ਸੀ।

ਜਦੋਂ ਮੈਂ ਦੋ ਸਾਲਾ ਦੀ ਸੀ ਉਦੋਂ ਮੈਂ ਆਪਣੇ ਪੂਹਰ ਨਾਲ
ਸ਼ੀ ਲੀਲਾ ਤੇ ਇੰਗਲੈਂਡ ਆਈ। ਉਸ ਵਕਤ ਮੇਰੇ ਪੂਹਰ ਵਿਚ ਮੇਰੇ
ਮਾਂ ਪਿਉ ਅਤੇ ਮੇਰੀ ਇਕ ਵਡੀ ਭੈਣ ਸੀ, ਜਿਹੜੀ ਮੇਰੇ ਤੋਂ ਸਾਢ
ਵਡੀ ਸੀ। ਅਸੀ ਦੀ ਲੰਮਾ ਤੇ ਸਿਧੇ ਲੰਡਨ ਆਏ ਜਿਥੇ ਸਾਢੇ ਬਹੁਤ
ਰਿਸ਼ਤੇਦਾਰ ਰਹਿੰਦੇ ਸਨ। ਇੰਗਲੈਂਡ ਵਿਚ ਮੇਰੇ ਦੋ ਹਰ ਦਾ ਜਨਮ
ਤੇ ਇਕ ਅਤੇ ਮੇਰਾ ਵਰਤਾਰ ਕਾਮ ਚਲਿਆ ਰਹਿ ਤਰ੍ਹਾਂ ਵਧਦੇ ਲਗਾ।
ਵਿਚ ਅਚਾਨਕ ਹੀ ਸਭ ਰੁਝ ਉਚਰੇਨ ਪੈ ਗਿਆ, ਤੇ ਮੇਰੇ ਪਿਤਾ ਜੀ
ਗੁਜਰ ਗਏ। ਉਸ ਵਕਤ ਮੇਰੀ ਉਮਰ ਜਾਂਹ ਸਾਲਾਂ ਦੀ ਸੀ। ਉਸ ਤੋਂ
ਵਾਰ ਮੇਰਾ ਵਰਤਾਰ ਮੇਰਾ ਪਾਰ ਪੌਜ਼ਨ ਕਾਮ ਜਿਵੇਂ ਚਲਿਆ ਦੀ
ਤਰ੍ਹਾਂ ਸਾ ਤੇ ਸਰਿਆ।

ਮਾਂ ਬੰਦੇ ਰੁਹੀਆਂ ਦੇ ਸਾਂਝੇ ਪੰਧਰੇਸ਼ਜ਼ਰ ਸਰੂਪ ਵਿਚ ਗਈ
ਜਿਥੇ ਮੈਂ ਵਹੁਤ ਸਾਰੀਆਂ ਅੰਗਰੇਜ਼ ਅਤੇ ਦੇਸ਼ਰ ਵਿਤਰੀਕਾਰ ਸਤੇਲੀਆ
ਵਹਤਾਇਆ। ਜਦੋਂ ਮੈਂ ਪੰਦਰਾਂ ਸਾਲਾ ਦੀ ਸੀ ਉਦੋਂ ਮੈਂ ਆਪਣਿਆ
ਸਤੇਲੀਆ ਨਾਲ ਅੰਦਰ ਵਾਹਰ ਜਾਣਾ ਸੁਰੂ ਕਰ ਦਿਤਾ। ਮੇਰਾ ਵਿਚ
ਕਰਨਾ ਸੀ ਕਿ ਮੈਂ ਵੀ ਸਰੂਪ ਵਿਤਸ਼ਕ ਵਿਚ ਜਾਂਦਾ, ਪਰ ਇਹ ਮੇਰੀ ਮਾਂ
ਨੂੰ ਵਿਚਰਣ ਪਸੰਦ ਨਹੀਂ ਸੀ। ਅਸਲ ਵਿਚ ਮੈਨੂੰ ਆਪਣੀ ਮਾਂ ਦੀ
ਤੋਰੀ ਪਸਦਾ ਨਹੀਂ ਸੀ। ਮੈਨੂੰ ਰਹੀ ਇਹ ਜੱਚ ਵਿਤਾਰ ਵਿਚ ਨਹੀਂ
ਆਇਆ ਸੀ, ਕਿ ਮੇਰੀ ਵਿਤਾਰੀ ਮਾਂ ਵਿਤਰਤੀਆਂ ਸੁਸਰਣਾ ਦਾ
ਸੁਰਘੇਰਾ ਕਰ ਕੇ, ਵਿਤਸ਼ਰਿਆ ਕਾਰ ਵਚਿਆਂ ਨੂੰ ਪਾਲ ਰਹੀ ਹੈ।

ਮੇਰੇ ਵਿਚ ਵਿਚ ਕਦੀ ਖਿਆਲ ਆਵੇ, ਮੇਰਾ ਵਿਚ
ਕਰਨਾ ਸੀ, ਰਾਮ ਕਿ ਮੇਰਾ ਰੰਗ ਦੀ ਜੋਰਾ ਰੁੰਦਾ, ਅਤੇ ਮੈਨੂੰ
ਦੀ ਆਪਣੀਆਂ ਸੇਹੇਲੀਆਂ ਵੇਸਰਾ ਨਾਲ ਅੰਦਰ ਵਾਹਰ ਜਾਣ
ਦੀ ਅਜ਼ਾਦੀ ਹੁੰਦੀ। ਮੇਰਾ ਵਿਚ ਕਰਨਾ ਸੀ, ਰਾਮ ਕਿ ਮੈਂ
ਦੇਸ਼ੀਕਾਰ ਦਾ ਹੁੰਦੀ, ਮੈਨੂੰ ਇਸ ਤਰ੍ਹਾਂ ਪੂਰੀਤ ਹੁੰਦਾ ਕਿ ਮੈਂ
ਦੇਸ਼ੀਕਾਰ ਤੇ ਕਰਕੇ ਮੈਂ ਆਪਣੇ ਸੇਹੇਲੀਆਂ ਵੇਸਰਾ ਨੂੰ ਨਾ-
ਪਸੰਦ ਹਾਂ। ਉਹ ਨੂੰ ਮੇਰਾ ਖਾਣਾ, ਪਾਣਾ ਸਭ ਰੁਝ ਨਾ-ਪਸੰਦ ਰਹਿ
ਮੇਰੇ ਰਖਣੇ ਸੇਜਰਾਬੀ ਕਰ, ਮੇਰੀ ਚੌਲੀ ਸੇਜਰਾਬੀ ਨੂੰ, ਰਾਬੇ
ਖਾਣੇ ਵਿਚੋਂ ਦੋ ਆਵੇਲੀ ਹੈ। ਮੈਨੂੰ ਇਹ ਸਾਰੀਆਂ ਗਲਾਂ ਉਰੀਆਂ
ਤੇ ਮੇਰਾ ਵਿਚ ਕਰਨਾ ਕਿ ਰਾਮ ਮੈਂ ਦੇਸ਼ੀਕਾਰ ਨਾ ਹੁੰਦੀ।

−7−

ਜਦੋ ਮੈਂ ਆਠਾਂਕ, ਉਨੀਆਂ ਸਾਲਾ ਦੀ ਹੋਈ, ਮੇਰੇ
ਵਿਆਹਾ ਦਾ ਰੁਕ ਤਹਿਰੀਕਾ ਆ ਗਈ। ਮੈਂ ਆਪਣੇ ਪੁਰਾ
ਤੇ ਉਨ੍ਹਾ ਦੀ ਕੌਮੀਆ ਵਿਚ ਤਰ-ਵੀਤੀ ਤੋ ਬਾਹੀ ਰੁਕ ਜ਼ਿਮੀਦਾਰਾ।
ਹਰ ਮੈਂ ਆਪਣੇ ਰਹਿਣੇ, ਪਹਿਣੇ ਅਤੇ ਆਪਣੀ ਸਭਿਆਤਾ ਵਿਚ
ਚਹਤ ਵਿਸ਼ਵਾਸਪਤੀ ਝੋ ਦ ਦਸ ਪਤੀ ਮੈਂ ਲੋ ਬੋਹੀ ਪਰਦਾ ਕਰੀ ਸਾੀ
ਕਿ ਮੇਰਾ ਹੀਸ ਗੌਰਾ ਰਹੀ। ਮੈਂ ਆਪਣੇ ਆਪ ਤੋ ਪੁਛਦੀ ਕਿ ਗੌਰਾ
ਹੀਸਾ ਹਰ ਵਿਚ ਕਿਹਦੀ ਮਹਤਤਾ ਹੈ? ਮੇਰਾ ਉਤਰ ਹਮੇਸ਼ਾ ਵਿਚ ਹੁੰਦਾ
ਕਿ ਇਸ ਵਿਚ ਕੋਈ ਮਹਤਤਾ ਨਹੀ। ਵਿਚ ਵਿਚ ਮੈਂ ਰਚ ਦਾ ਸੁਕਰ-
ਗੁਜ਼ਾਰ ਹੁੰਦੀ, ਕਿ ਮੈਂ ਉਤਰੇ ਵਰੇ ਪਰਦਾਰ ਵਿਚੋ ਆਈ ਜਾਂ ਜੋ ਇਕ
ਦੂਜੇ ਨੂੰ ਪਿਆਰ ਕਰਦੇ ਹਨ ਤੇ ਸਗਰਾ ਵਿਚੋ ਹਨ। ਸਾਰੇ ਵਿਸ਼ਤੇਦਾਰ
ਮੈਨੂੰ ਅਤੇ ਮੇਰੇ ਭੈਣਾਂ ਭਰਾਵਾਂ ਨਾਲ ਵਿਸ ਤਰਾਂ ਦਾ ਦਰਤਾ ਕਰਦੇ ਸਨ, ਜਿਸ
ਤਰਾਂ ਕਿ ਸਗਲ ਉਨ੍ਹਾ ਦੇ ਆਪਣੇ ਸਕੇ ਧੀਆਂ, ਪੁਤਰ ਹੋਵੇ। ਮੇਰਾ ਆਪਣਾ
ਰਹੇਰੇ ਹੋਦਾ ਭਰਾਵਾਂ ਨਾਲ ਚਹਤ ਸਗਰਾ ਰਗੜਾ ਹੋਦਾ, ਤੇ ਹਰ ਮੈਂ ਉਨ੍ਹਾ
ਨਾਲ ਜੀ ਅੰਜਕ ਚਾਰ ਜਾਂਦੀ। ਵਿਚ ਸਭ ਰੂਪ ਮੇਰੀ ਮਾਂ ਨੂੰ ਚਹਤ ਪਸੰਦ
ਸੀ।

ਜੇ ਸਕਰ ਹਰ ਮੈਂ ਘਰ ਕਾੀ ਰਹਿੰਦੀ, ਪਰ ਹਰ ਤਹਿਰੀਤਰ
ਸੌਹਦਰਾ ਨੂੰ ਆਪਣੀ ਮਾਂ ਨੂੰ ਸਿਸ਼ਟ ਜਾਂਦੀ ਜਾਂ, ਮੈਂ ਆਪਣੇ
ਰਾਹੇ ਦੇ ਧੀਆਂ, ਪੁਤਰਾ ਨੂੰ ਵੀ ਸਿਸ਼ਟੀ, ਜਦੂਰੀ ਜਾਂ, ਮੈਂ ਆਪਣੀ
ਮਾਂ ਸਮੇ ਵਿਚ ਸਿਧ ਰਹਿਤਾ ਕਾਰੀਵੀ ਜਾਂ ਕਿ ਘਰ ਤੋਂ ਦੂਰਾਰ
ਹੋਣ ਵਿਚ ਕੋਈ ਗਲਤੀ ਰਾਹੀ ਹਾਲ ਨਹੀ। ਮੈਂ ਘਰ ਤੋ
ਦੂਰਾਰ ਵਿਸ ਕਰਕੇ ਰਹ ਨਹੀ ਜਾਂ ਕਿ ਘਰ ਵਿਚ ਮੇਰਾ ਪੜਾਈ
ਰਸਤਾ ਚਹਤ ਸਸਰਕ ਨੇ ਵਿਉਂਕਿ ਮੇਰੇ ਹੋ ਰੁਕ ਚਹਤ ਜੌਰ
ਪਾਉਦੇ ਹਨ ਅਤੇ ਹਰ ਹੋਸ ਸਹੀਸਾਰ ਆਖੇ ਰਹਿੰਦੇ ਹਨ। ਸਦੇ ਕਈ
ਰਹੇਰੇ ਹੋਦ ਰੁਕ ਘਦੇ ਚਾਰਰ ਘੁਰਰਦਰਜ਼ੀ ਵਿਚ ਪੜੁਦੇ ਹਨ,
ਜਾ ਪੜੁਦੇ ਰਹ ਹਨ। ਵਿਸ ਕਰਕੇ ਮੇਰਾ ਚਾਰਰ ਰਹਿਤ ਰ
ਕਿਸੇ ਨੂੰ ਕੋਈ ਇਤਰਾਜ਼ ਨਹੀ। ਹਰ ਮੈਂ ਵਿੰਨ ਸਾਰ ਨੂੰ
ਘਰੇ ਚਾਰ ਰਹ ਰਹੀ ਜਾਂ, ਜ਼ਾਹਿਰ ਸੇ ਮੈਂ ਹਰ ਘਰ ਦਖਸ਼
ਜਾ ਰੇ ਮਾਂ ਕੋਰ ਰਹਾ। ਵਿਉਂਕਿ ਜਦੇ ਮੈਂ ਘਰ ਆਪਣੀ ਮਾਂ
ਕੋਰ ਜਾਂਦੀ ਜਾਂ, ਉਹ ਸਮੇ ਦੀ ਮੈਂ ਨੂੰ ਚਹਤ ਸਮਝਦੇ ਹੈ,
ਸਦੇ ਵਿਚ ਮੈਂ ਨੂੰ ਪਸੰਦ ਨਹੀ ਆਦਾ ਅਤੇ ਸਾਡਾ ਝਗੜਾ ਤੋ ਜਾਂਦਾ

ਇਕ ਦਿਆ ਰੀ ਦੂਸਰੇ ਵਿਚ ਮੰਦੇ ਵਿਚ ਗਾਰ ਪਸੰਦ ਰੂ ਕਿ ਮੇਰੇ
ਜੁਮੇਦਾਰੀ ਮੇਰੇ ਜਿਮ ਤੇ ਹੈ। ਮੇਰੇ ਮਾਂ ਨੂੰ ਮੇਰ ਬਹੁਤ ਚਿੰਤਾ
ਸੀ ਮੇਰੇ ਵਿਆਜਗਾਰ ਵਿਆਜ ਵਿਚਰਨ ਪਸੰਦ ਰਾਂ। ਵੇਸ਼ਜਿਸ
ਮਾਪੇ ਆਪਣੇ ਵਾਲਿਆਂ ਨੂੰ ਆਪਣੇ ਤੋਂ ਆਜਾਰ ਹੋਣ ਵਿਚਰਨ
ਪਸੰਦ ਰਾਂ। ਜਿਗਰ ਉੱਦੇ ਹੀ ਵਾਲਿਆਂ ਨੂੰ ਘਰੋਂ ਵਾਹਰ ਜਾਣ
ਰੀ ਇਜਾਜਤ ਮਿਲਦੀ ਜੋ ਉਨ੍ਹਾਂ ਦਾ ਵਿਆਜ ਵੀ ਜਾਦੇ।

ਜਦੋ ਹੀ ਵਿਆਜ ਦਾ ਜੁਆਜਾਰ ਜਾਜਾਰ ਹੀ ਹੋਣ ਹੀ ਮੇਰ
ਮੇਰ ਮੇਰਾ ਮਾਂ ਨੂੰ ਰਗੜਾ ਰੂ ਜਾਗਾ ਹੀ। ਮਾਰੇ ਮੈਨੂੰ ਹੋਰੀ ਵਿਆਜ
ਰਰਨ ਤੇ ਜੋਰ ਰਾਂ ਪਾ ਵਿਰ, ਵਿਉਂਕਿ ਮਾਰੇ ਮੇਰ ਵਰੀ ਬੋਂਟ ਜਾਣਤ
ਕਿ ਸਰੂਰੀ ਜਾਣ ਵੀ ਜ ਵੇਸਮ ਰੂ, ਮਾਰੇ ਰੁਮਾਰੇ ਹੀ। ਮੇਰੇ ਵਿਆਜਦੇ ਵਿਚ
ਕਿ ਸਾਰੀਆਂ ਹੋਣਾਂ ਬੋਂਟ ਹੋਣ ਰਾ ਵਿਆਜ ਆਪਣੇ ਰਜਮ ਵਿਰਾਜ ਰਾਰ,
ਰਾਂ ਤੇ ਰੰਗਾ। ਮਾਜਮ ਹੋਣੇ ਪਹੁਜੀ ਕਿਜਮ ਦੇ ਵਿਆਜ ਨੂੰ ਪਸੰਦ
ਰਰਦੀਆਂ ਜਾਂ। ਮਾਜਰ ਵਿਚ ਦਿਨ ਦਿਨ ਉਚਾਈ ਦੇ ਜਾਰ ਹੀ। ਮੈਂ
ਰਹੇ ਦਿਨ ਰਹੀ ਰਾਜੀਵਾ ਜਾ ਕਿ ਮੈਨੂੰ ਪਹੁਜੀ ਮਾਰੇ ਵੇਸ਼ਮਾਜ ਰਰਜਮ
ਵਿਰਾਜਾ ਵਿਵੇਂ ਵਿਚ ਬਹੁਤਾ ਪਦੇ। ਮੈਨੂੰ ਜਿਗਰ ਵਿਤਪਤਾ ਹੀ ਕਿ ਜਾਂ.
ਆਪਣੇ ਮਨ-ਪਸੰਦ ਮਾਰਜਮ ਜਾਰ, ਵਿਆਜ ਰਰਦਤਾ ਜਾਰੂਰੀ ਤਾਂ ਬੋਂਟੇ
ਉਂ ਜੰਜ ਹੇਰੇ ਜਾ ਰਾਜਾ। ਸੁਵਿਰ ਮੇਰ ਪੂਰਜ ਰਹੇ ਜਾਰ ਦੋਰੂਰਾ
ਬੈਂਰ ਲੇਰੇ। ਮੈਂ ਇਹ ਰਾਂ ਰਾਜੂਰੀ ਕਿ ਜਾਂਜਾ ਤੇ, ਵਿਉਂਕਿ ਜਾਂਨੂੰ
ਆਪਣੇ ਪੂਰਜ ਰਾਰੂ, ਪਤਹ ਪਿਆਰ ਹੈ। ਸੁਵਿਰ ਜਾਂ ਰਹਰੀ ਰੀ ਵਿਆਜ
ਰਾ ਰਗੜੇ।

ਰਰ ਮੇਰ ਵਿਆਜ ਮੇਰ ਪਰੂਹੀ ਜਗ ਮੇਰ ਰੈਮ-ਰਹੇ
ਇਰੇ ਹੀ, ਵਿਆਜ ਰਾ ਜਾਂ ਨੂੰ ਬੋਰ ਬੋ ਵਿਆਜ ਰਾਂ। ਜਾਂ.ਰਾਂ
ਰਾਜੂੰਰੀ ਕਿ ਮੇਰ ਪੂਰਜ ਵਿਰਾ ਗਾਰਾ ਵਿਚ ਬੋਰੀ ਰਾਬ ਰੇਰੇ, ਰਾਂ ਹੀ
ਜਾਂ ਉਨ੍ਹਾਂ ਨੂੰ ਰਹਰ ਰੰਦ ਰਹਾਂਗੀ।

                                              ਇਕਬਾਲ.

NO MONEY IN MY HAND

My mother's heart will break if she come to know or see my life here today. I was very special to my mother among her four children. I was brought up under Muslim religion. I had to stop my school at age of 12 years. I lived in Boroda, my father had a soap shop—we were not poor, compare to the lots of people in India we were not short of food and clothing. At 19, I had to get married to my cousin. My father was very happy about this marriage as he was in England earning lots of money. My mother was against this marriage. Because sometimes he used to come to Boroda and stayed in our house. During those days he shouted at us for every little cause. I did not mind that much though he is 15 years older than me, coming to England excited me more than anything else. When some of our cousins used to come and stay with us, we used to take them to see Hindi coloured film. All those films sing song in London, Paris, New York made a great impression on my mind. Still today very large number of Indian people look at England with high admiration. Those who manage to come here and their occasional gifts back home make quite a sensation. My husband is a religious man—he regrets always as he could not go for higher education and wants our children to become doctors. He works in a dress factory and always moans about it.

After I came here, all joy and dream disappeared. I felt lost, really completely lost. At airport, looking all around me so many people and so much things happening—still today I can't explain that confusion. All the way from airport first by tube and then by bus to his Stoke Newington bed–sitter. Worse to come carrying heavy bags. I started to realise my husband is very mean though he impresses family back home with gifts. He helped me first few days how to use gas, shops and laundry etc. He always talked about money how much someone can earn here. Because of my lack of English I started to feel very unhappy—I did not have any friend either. Whole day I cried, on top of it my husband come home and showed his temper and beat me up even. He is very unhappy at his work. He felt better when I started to make dresses at home. All day long making dresses then cooking good Indian meal, again sit down with machine—I really feel like commiting suicide—but I am now pregnant. We moved to a council flat near Whitechapel Market. It is one of those old block of flats on the ground floor. Group of 11/12 years boys broke one of our windows. I could hear from inside shouting calling Paki, Blacki, etc. My husband could not take it anymore. One day he slapped the leader of the gang and took him to his mother next block.

After that incident they quieten down a lot. Salim was born. Still I feel very lonely and no friend—my husband does not want me to mix with other Indian/Pakistani people I meet at Halal meat shop/market. All my relative live at Leicester. My husband came to know about a drop−in centre for women and under 5, from clinic. For my English he took me there with baby. Though I don't speak and understand English they accepted me very nicely. Everybody try to talk to me and love Salim. I feel happy when I go there. Now I understand a bit more English and can say one or two sentences. I want to speak English but think always I will be wrong. I have got another girl now Nargis. It is so hard managing on my own shopping, cooking, laundry also whenever my husband can get some work to make dresses he bring it at home. He only thinks of money and food never thinks or treats me as human. I know lots of women like me only get used for earning money and keeping home. I have no money in my hand. Being in England I am able to earn at home and being Indian I have no right on my own earning. I cannot revolt it will cause lot of unpleasantness in the family. He is my Uncle's son. I can't talk about it. I don't want to shatter my father's dream 'I am happy and well off here'. Man get money mad after coming here.

Now I think all these unhappiness and pressure showing on Salim— he is more than 3 years—he is not talking and behind for his age. For me now only I can see more unhappiness—I wish I was in India just as I was.

PARVEEN'

પરવીન   'પૈસાની અછત'

મારા આજના રોજિંદા જીવનની ઢબ જો મારી માના
જાણવા કે જોવામાં આવે તો એના દિલને ખૂબ દુઃખ થાય.
અમારા ભાઈબહેનોમાં હું મારી માની ખાસ માનીતી દિકરી હતી.
મારો ઉછેર મુસ્લીમ (ઈસ્લામ) ધર્મની રૂઢિ પ્રમાણે થયો હતો. બાર વર્ષની
ઉંમરે મારે શાળા છોડી દેવી પડી હતી. હું બરોડા (ગુજરાત)માં રહેતી હતી.
મારા પિતાની સાબુની દુકાન હતી. અમે ગરીબ વર્ગમાં લેખાતા ન હતા.
ભારતના ઘણા બધા લોકોની જેમ અમને ખાવાપીવાની કોઈ ખોટ ન હતી.
ઓગણીસ (૧૯) વર્ષની ઉંમરે મારા પિત્રાય ભાઈ (cousin) સાથે મારા લગ્ન
થયા. મારા પિતાને આ લગ્નનો ખૂબ આનંદ હતો કારણ કે મારા પતિ
ઈંગ્લેન્ડમાં રહેતા હતા અને એમની કમાણી પણ ઘણી સારી હતી. મારી મા આ
લગ્નની વિરોધી હતી. કારણ કે મારા પતિ પહેલા ઘણીવાર મારે ઘેર બરોડા
આવ્યા હતા ત્યારે નજીવા કારણોસર પણ તેઓ મારા કુટુંબીજનો સાથે
ગુસ્સે થતા જે મારી માને જરાય પસંદ ન હતું. મારા પતિની ઉંમર મારા
કરતા પંદર વર્ષ મોટી હતી. છતાં એનો મને જરાપણ અફસોસ ન હતો.
ઈંગ્લેન્ડ આવવાની ઉમળકો મને બીજા બધાં કરતા વધારે ઉત્સાહિત કરતો
હતો. જ્યારે પણ અમારા પિત્રાય ભાઈબેનો (cousins) અમારે ત્યાં રજાઓમાં
રહેવા આવતા ત્યારે અમે એમને હિંદી રંગીન ફિલ્મો જોવા લઈ જતા.
આ ફિલ્મોમાં લંડન, પેરિસ ન્યુયોર્ક વગેરે પ્રખ્યાત મોટા શહેરોમાં
ફિલ્માવેલા ગીતો જોઈ તથા સાંભળીને એની મારા પર મોટી અસર થઈ
હતી. આજે પણ ભારતના ઘણા બધા લોકો ઈંગ્લેન્ડ વિષે ઊંચા વિચારો
ધરાવે છે. નસીબજોગે જેઓ ઈંગ્લેન્ડમાં આવીને વસતા તેઓ પ્રસંગોપાત
ભારતના સગાસ્નેહીઓને જે ભેટસોગાદો મોકલાવે છે એનું ભારતમાં
ખૂબ મહત્વ ગણાય છે.
મારા પતિ ધાર્મિકવૃત્તિના વ્યક્તિ છે. પોતાને વધુ અભ્યાસ
કરવાની તક મળી ન હતી એનો એમને હંમેશા અફસોસ થાય છે. એમની
ઘણી ઇચ્છા છે કે અમારા બાળકો ભણીગણીને ભવિષ્યમાં ડોક્ટર બને.
મારા પતિ ફેક્ટરીમાં નોકરી કરે છે પણ એ કામમાં એ ખુશ નથી.
આ દેશમાં આવ્યા પછી મારો બધો આનંદ અને ઉમળકો શમી
ગયો. હું જાણે ખોવાઈ ગઈ હોઉ એવું જ મને લાગ્યું. લંડનના લીધા
એરપોર્ટ પર લોકોની ધમાલ અને હસલબસલથી હું ડઘાઈ જ ગઈ.
તે વખતની મારા મનની મૂંઝવણ હું આજે પણ શબ્દોમાં સમજાવી શકતી
નથી. એરપોર્ટથી પહેલા ટ્યુબ ટ્રેનમાં અને પછી બસમાં મુસાફરી કરીને
અમે સ્ટોક ન્યુઈંગ્ટનના અમારા બેડસીટ રૂમ પર પહોંચ્યા. પોતાની
વજનદાર બેગો ઉંચકવાનું મને બહુ મુશ્કેલ લાગ્યું. ધીરે ધીરે મને લાગવા
માંડ્યુ કે મારા પતિ બહુ સંકુચિત માનસના હતા. માત્ર અવારનવાર મારા
ભારતના સગાંઓને ભેટો મોકલીને પ્રભાવિત કરતા હતા. અહીં આવ્યા પછી
શરૂઆતમાં ગેસ કેવી રીતે વાપરવો, દુકાનોમાં કેવી રીતે જવું તથા કપડા ધોવા
માટે લોન્ડ્રીના મશીનનો કેવી રીતે ઉપયોગ કરવો વગેરે બાબતો મારા
પતિએ મને શીખવી.

-12-

મારા પતિ હંમેશા પૈસા વિષે જ વાત કરે છે જે વ્યક્તિ કમાવા ચાહે તે આ દેશમાં ઘણી કમાણી કરી શકે છે. મને અંગ્રેજી ભાષા બરાબર આવડતી ન હોવાથી હું ખૂબ નાખુશ થવા લાગી. મારી કોઈ સહેલી પણ ન હતી. ઘણીવાર હું આખો દિવસ રડતી હતી. અધૂરામાં પૂરુ મારા પતિ સાંજે ઘરે આવીને મારા પર ગુસ્સે થઈ મને મારતા પણ હતા. પોતાની નોકરીમાં સરખાય ન હોવાથી એ કામમાં ખુશ નથી. ધીરે ધીરે મેં પણ ઘેર ડ્રેસ સીલાવવનું કામ શરૂ કર્યું ને મારા પતિને ઘણું ગમ્યું. આખો દિવસ હું સીલાયનું કામ કરતી, સાંજે આખી ગુજરાતી રસોઈ કરતી અને જમીપરવારી ઘરનું કામકાજ પતાવીને પાછું હું સીવવાનું કામ કરવા બેસતી. આ પ્રકારના ઓચિંતા કામ્મુમથી હું ખરેખર ખૂબ કંટાળી ગઈ હતી. ઘણીવાર આત્મહત્યા કરવાનું પણ મને મન થઈ આવતું. હવે હું પ્રેગનન્ટ (સગર્ભા) છું. લાયન સેપમ માર્કેટની બાજુમાં કાઉન્સિલના ફ્લેટમાં અમે રહીએ છીએ. અમારો બ્લોક બહુ જૂનો છે. અમે ગ્રાઉન્ડ ફ્લોર પર રહીએ છીએ. અનેકવાર દસ બાર વર્ષની ઉંમરના કેટલાંક છોકરાઓએ અમારી બારી તોડી નાંખી હતી. બહારથી તેઓ 'પાકી' 'કાળિયા' એવા શબ્દો જોર જોરથી બોલે છે તે હું મારા ઘરમાં સાંભળી શકું છું. મારા પતિ આ બધું વધારે સહન કરી શક્યા નહિ. એક દિવસ એ ગ્રુપના નેતાને પકડીને એને એક ધબ્બક મારીને એની મા પાસે બાજુના બ્લોકમાં લઈ ગયા હતા. આ બનાવ પછી છોકરાઓની કનડગત ઘણી ઓછી થઈ ગઈ છે.

થોડા વખત પછી મારા પુત્ર સલીમનો જન્મ થયો. છતું પણ મને ઘણું એકલવાયું લાગે છે. મારી કોઈ સહેલી નથી. છતાં મીટની દુકાનમાં કે સુપર માર્કેટમાં બીજા ઈન્ડિયન કે પાકિસ્તાની બૈરાં સાથે બાબુ એ મારા પતિને પસંદ ન હતું. મારા બધાં સગાસ્નેહીઓ લેસ્ટરમાં રહે છે. ક્લીનિકમાં અવારનવાર જતા પાંચ વર્ષની નીચેની ઉંમરના બાળકોનું તથા સ્ત્રીઓ માટેના એક કેન્દ્રની ભાળ મારા પતિને થઈ. મારા બાળક સાથે આ કેન્દ્રમાં હું અંગ્રેજી ભાષા શીખવા માટે જતી. અંગ્રેજી બોલતા કે સમજતા મને જરાપણ આવડતું ન હતું છતાં એ કેન્દ્રના બાઈઓને મને ખૂબ સારો આવકાર આપ્યો. ત્યાંના બધાં મારી સાથે ખૂબ વાતચીત કરે છે. તેમને સલીમ પણ ખૂબ ગમે છે. આ કેન્દ્રમાં જવાથી મને ખૂબ આનંદ મળે છે. હવે હું અંગ્રેજી ભાષા વધારે પ્રમાણમાં સમજ શકું છું અને એકબે વાક્યો અંગ્રેજીમાં બોલી પણ શકું છું. અંગ્રેજી બોલવાનો મને ખૂબ શોખ છે પણ મને ધ્રા કરે છે કે હું હંમેશા ખોટે અંગ્રેજી બોલું છું.

મારે હવે બીજી દીકરી છે. એનું નામ નરગીસ છે. ઘરનું બધું કામકાજ, ખરીદી, રસોઈ લોન્ડ્રી તથા બાળકોની સંભાળ આ બધાને મારા એકલા હાથે પણ્હોંચી વળવું મને બહુ મુશ્કેલ લાગે છે. ઘણીવાર મારા પતિને ફેક્ટરીમાંથી કામ મળે ત્યારે મારે મારે પણ ઘેર ડ્રેસ સીવવાનું કામ લઈ આવે છે. એમના મનમાં પૈસા અને ખાવાનું આ બે બાબતો જ હંમેશા તરસ્સેલી હોય છે.

તેઓ મને એક વ્યક્તિ તરીકે સમજવાનો પ્રયાસ જ કરતા નથી. મારા જેવી બીજી ઘણી સ્ત્રીઓને હું જાણું છું કે જેઓ મારી જેમ ઘર ચલાવવા તથા પૈસા કમાવવાના હેતુથી જ જીવન જીવે છે. મારા હાથમાં પૈસા હોતા નથી. ઇંગ્લેન્ડમાં હોવાથી હું ઘેર બેઠા કામ કરીને પૈસા કમાઈ શકું છું પરંતુ એક ભારતીય મહિલા તરીકે મને મારી કમાઈના પૈસા પર કોઈ અધિકાર નથી. આ બાબતનો હું વિરોધ કરી શકતી નથી. જો એમ કરવા પ્રયત્ન કરું તો ઘરમાં ઘણા ઝઘડા કજીયા ઊભા થાય. મારા પતિ મારા ઘરનો દીકરો થાય તેથી એના વિષે હું કાંઈ કહી શકું નહિ.

મારા માતાપિતાનું સ્થાન હું ઉઘાડવા માંગતી નથી. તેઓ માને છે તેમ હું અહીં 'સુખી' અને 'સંતોષી' છું. આ દેશમાં આવ્યા પછી માણસો પૈસા પાછળ ગાંડા બની જાય છે. હવે મને લાગે છે કે મારી નાખુશી તથા રોજિંદા જીવનના ભારની ખરાબ અસર સલીમના જીવન પર પણ પડી છે. એ ત્રણ વર્ષની ઉંમરનો છે છતાં બોલી શકતો નથી અને એની ઉંમરના બીજાં બાળકો કરતા પછાત છે. મારા પોતા માટે મને વધારે ને વધારે નાખુશી અને અસંતોષ જ દેખાય છે. ઘણીવાર મને થાય છે કે હું ભારતમાં જ હોત તો કેવું સારૂં!

THE GIRL HAS GOT BRAINS

I am 16 years old. I live in London. My parents come from India in Bombay. I was born over here and have been here since. I have never seen India but I am hoping to go next year after I've given my exams. I have got 2 brothers and 2 sisters. 1 sister is married with 3 kids, 1 brother is married with 2 kids and the other sister is engaged. She's going to get married next year.

Now I want to tell you about myself. I will tell you the truth. People reckon it is wrong for Muslim or Asian girls to have boyfriends well I for one think it is very silly, because I have got a boyfriend. You see I've been going out with him for 8 months now and during that time I had got caught twice. First time I got caught I got in to a lot of trouble then when I got caught again me and my parents had a big fight you know what they said to me, they said I can't go to school anymore, I must sit at home and work. I pleaded with them and so in the end they had agreed with me so long as I don't see that boy again. So now I am back to school and I am still seeing that boy. You want to know why, because I love him and I just want to be with him. Why is it that parents don't like their daughters to go out with a boy? Well I think that Asian parents think that if they do let their daughters go out with boys, their daughters might jump into bed with the boy, but I think that is wrong and of course the girl has got brains. I don't think she'll just jump into bed with a guy.

If the Asian parents don't give enough freedom to the girl she is bound to do just what her parents don't want her to do, and I also think we should be able to marry the person we love not the person who our parents think is suitable. We should not have arranged marriages after all this is not the old days, the past. But this is the present with the new generation not the old generation. You might think I am being silly to go out with this boy the 3rd time but I am not being silly because I know what I am doing. He is the first boy I have fallen in love with. Why can't my parents just accept the fact that I love him and no one will stop me seeing him unless I die. Until then I won't stop seeing him. I have tried to talk about him but they won't listen, they think they know what is best for me. I have listened to what they had to say so now why can't they listen to what I've got to say, and the only other person I can talk to is my sister—in—law. She understands me and gives me good advice. Apart from her I don't think I could turn to anyone.

NARGIS

लड़की भी दिमाग़ रखती है

मेरी आयु १६ वर्ष है। मैं लन्दन में रहती हूं।
मेरे माता-पिता भारत (बम्बई) से आये हैं। मैंने यहां
जन्म लिया और जब से अब तक मैं यहां रह रही
हूं। मैंने भारत कभी नहीं देखा किन्तु मैं आशा करती
हूं कि अगले वर्ष परीक्षा समाप्त होने पर मैं वहां जाऊंगी।
मेरी दो बहिनें और दो भाई हैं। एक बहिन की शादी हो
चुकी है और उनके तीन बच्चे हैं। एक भाई की भी शादी
हो चुकी है और उनके दो बच्चे हैं। मेरी दूसरी बहिन
की भी सगाई हो चुकी है और अगले वर्ष उनकी शादी
हो जायेगी।

अब मैं अपने सम्बन्ध में कुछ बताना चाहती हूं। जो कि
सच होगा। लोगों का विचार है कि एक मुस्लिम या राशियन
लड़की के लिए यह उचित नहीं कि वह किसी लड़के को
अपना मित्र बनाये। पर मेरे विचार में इसा सोचना मूर्खता है
क्योंकि मेरी एक लड़के से मित्रता है। मैं लगभग आठ महीने
से उसके साथ बाहर जा रही हूं। और इस बीच में दो
बार पकड़ी गयी हूं। पहली बार जब मैं पकड़ी गयी तो
मुझे बड़ी कठिनाईयों का सामना करना पड़ा। और जब मैं दोबारा
पकड़ी गयी तो मुझमें और मेरे माता-पिता में एक प्रकार
का युद्ध छिड़ गया। अब्बा कहना था कि अब मैं स्कूल
नहीं जा सकती हूं और मुझे घर ही में रहकर काम
करना होगा। मैंने किसी प्रकार से उन्हें मना लिया और

अन्त में वह इस शर्त पर सहमत हो गये कि मैं स्कूल जा सकती हूँ अगर मैं उस लड़के से ना मिलूँ। अतः अब मैं स्कूल जा रही हूँ और उस लड़के से भी मिल रही हूँ। आप जानना चाहते हैं क्यों? क्योंकि मैं उससे प्रेम करती हूँ और उसके साथ रहना चाहती हूँ। वजह क्यों है कि मेरे माता-पिता को यह पसन्द नहीं है कि उनकी लड़की किसी लड़के के साथ बाहर जाये? मेरे विचार से रशियन माता-पिता यह सोचते हैं कि यदि उन्होंने अपनी लड़की को किसी लड़के के साथ घूमने-फिरने जाने की आज्ञा दी तो वह लड़की उसके साथ सीधी बिस्तर में चली जायेगी। परन्तु मेरे विचार से यह गलत है, क्योंकि लड़की को भी तो दिमाग़ होता है। यह बिल्कुल गलत है कि एक लड़की किसी लड़के के साथ बिस्तर में छलांग लगा देगी।

यदि रशियन माता-पिता अपनी लड़की को उचित पर्याप्त स्वतन्त्रता नहीं देते हैं तो वह वह सब करने को फिर बाध्य हो जायेगी जो कि माता-पिता की दृष्टि कोण से उसे नहीं करना चाहिए। और मैं यह भी सोचती हूँ कि हमें यह अनुमति मिलनी चाहिए कि हम उस व्यक्ति से शादी कर सकें जिससे हम प्रेम करते हैं, न कि उससे जिसके बारे में हमारे माता-पिता सोचते हैं कि वह दरअसल हमारी लड़की के लिए उचित है। और यह कोई ज़रूरी बात तो है ही नहीं कि हमारे माता-पिता

द्वारा चुने गये व्यक्ति से शादी करें। क्योंकि आज का युग वर्तमान युग है और नई पीढ़ी। हो सकता है आप यह सोच रहे हों कि मैं उस लड़के से मिलकर मूर्खता कर रही हूँ, परन्तु मैं यह जानती हूँ कि मैं जो कुछ कर रही हूँ वह सही कर रही हूँ। वह पहला लड़का है जिसे मैं प्रेम करती हूँ। क्यों नहीं मेरे माता-पिता यह मानने को तैयार होते हैं कि मुझे उससे प्रेम है और कोई भी मुझे उससे मिलने से नहीं रोक सकता। सिवाये इसके मैं मर जाऊँ। इसके अतिरिक्त कोई भी वस्तु मुझे उससे मिलने से नहीं रोक सकती। मैंने इस सम्बन्ध में उनसे बात करने का प्रयास किया पर वह सुनते ही नहीं। वह सोचते हैं कि उन्हें यह पता है कि मेरे लिए क्या उचित है। वे जो कुछ कहना चाहते थे मैंने सुना तो वे क्यों नहीं सुनते जो कुछ मैं कहना चाहती हूँ? मेरी भाभी केवल ऐसी हैं जिनसे मैं इस सम्बन्ध में बात कर सकती हूँ. वह मेरी बात समझती हैं मुझे परामर्श देती हैं। उनके सिवाय कोई भी ऐसा नहीं है जिससे मैं ~~अपनी~~ परामर्श कर सकूँ।

नरगीस

TO THINK THAT I COULD EVER BE LIVE HERE

I was born in India. When I was 17 I came to England with my brother and mother because my father was here.

The life of England is completely different from India. When I came here I found it very strange. It was difficult to think I could ever be live here. The things I missed very much were language, culture, dress, food, friends, school life. I miss the chat food sometime used to have on my way from school.

Me and my brother knew English reading and writing but not speaking. So my brother joined ESL class but it was a mixed class so I wasn't allowed to go although I loved to go there. Sometimes later I found a class only for women so I joined that class. I've found a class but I couldn't find a friend. There are a lot of women but not a girl. I don't want a woman friend with children, because when they come to my home looks like they are my mum's friends instead of mine. My mum give them advice about their children that what to do and what not to do and so, and I just don't like these things.

Now my brother have been going to college. But I am still not allowed to go to College because of my culture. Anyhow, I am not brave enough to put pressure on my parents but I am involving them to allow me to go to the college. They know I feel lonely and I think that I am wasting my time. I don't feel very happy, they are worried about me, but they are not ready enough to allow me to do whatever I want.

In my opinion I think that the parents or fathers who want to settle in this country should call over their children in young age, that they won't feel strange here.

NASEEM

آج کل میرا چھوٹا کالج جا رہا ہے مگر مجھے کالج جانے کی اجازت نہیں
ہے ۔ لیکن میرے میں میرے اندر اتنی ہمت ہے کہ نہ تک یہ تھوڑا تھوڑا دباؤ؟ ڈالوں
میں آہستہ آہستہ اپنی اس طرف لانے کی کوشش کرتی ہوں ۔ اپنی ایک اس
چیز کا اندازہ ہے کہ میں یہاں تنہائی محسوس کرتی ہوں اور میرے وقت کی
برمادی کا احساس ہے ۔ وہ اس بارے میں فکرمند رہتے ہیں ۔ مگر وہ
سب کچھ کرنے کی اجازت نہیں دیتے جو کہ میں کرنا چاہتی ہوں۔ لیکن ایک
نہ ایک دن وہ اس بات کا اقرار کریں گے اور مجھے اسی سے کہ مجھے اجازت مل
جائے گی ۔

اس معاملے میں میری دلی ہے کہ وہ والدین اپنی اولاد کو اس ملک میں
مستقل رہائش کے لئے بلانا چاہتے ہیں اپنی چاہئے کہ وہ کم عمری میں ہی اپنے
بچوں کو یہاں بلا لیں تاکہ وہ کسی ذہنیت کا شکار نہ ہوں۔

نسیم

یہ خیال مند میں سی سی یہاں رہ سکتی ہیں

میری بیرونی ہندوستان کی ہے ۔ جب میری عمر کا سال تقی نے میں
برطانیہ آئی - (اپنے عباؤ اور دادہ کے ساتھ) کیونک میرے والد یہاں
مقیم تھے۔

برطانیہ کی زندگی ہندوستان کی زندگی سے بہت مختلف ہے ۔ جب میں
یہاں آئی نے شروع شروع میں میں نے برٹی اجنبیت محسوس کی ۔ اس وقت
یہ سوچنا تھی مشکل تھا کہ میں سی سی یہاں رہ سکتی ہوں ۔ زبان، تہذیب
وتمدن، لباس، ،کا مکلواڑے ۔ ہست دانماب اور سکول کی زندگی یہ وہ چیزیں
تھیں میں کی سی طرح محسوس ہوا؟۔

مجھے اور میرے عباؤ کی انگریزی لکھی پڑھنی آتی تھی مگر بولنے سے ہم دولں
ہی قاصرتھے - لہذا میرے عباؤ نے اے۔ایس۔ایل (E.S.L) کی کلاسیں لینی شروع
کردیں ۔ باوجود بے استہا چاہنے کے مجھے وہاں جانے کی اجازت نہ مل سکی ۔ کیونک
وہ لڑکوں اور لڑکیوں کی ایک ملی جلی کلاس تھی۔ سچی ہی دلوں بعد مجھے ایک ایسے
کلاس کا پتہ لگا ۔ جو صرف خواتین کے لئے تھا۔ مجھے کلاس تو مل گئی مگر دوست
لپ تھی نہ مل سکی - کیونک وہاں لڑکی کوئ؟ ہیں ہیں سب عورتیں یا عورتیں ہیں۔
اور شادی شدہ بال بچوں والی عورتوں کو میں اپن دوست بنانا پند نہیں کرتی
۔ کیونک وہ جب اکثر سبی میرے گھر آتی ہیں تو مجھے زیادہ میری والدہ کی دوست نظر
آتی ہیں ۔ اور میری والدہ ماہم نہیں ان کے بچوں کے بارے ہیں ہرایات
دیتی دیتی ہیں کہ کیا کرنا چاہیے اور کیا نہیں؟ اور مجھے یہ دانمات
نم کی باتیں بلکل پند نہیں۔

WHAT MATTERS TO THE WORLD IS MONEY

It was in the 1960's when I was very small. I used to crawl, an 11 month old baby. I was in Pakistan. I used to live in a cottage, a very small cottage. It had very bad cement walls which looked like they were ready to drop down. The ceiling was flaky and at any time when there was a thunder, the small pieces used to float off and fall on anyone's head.

I used to think how my parents could live in such place. At one time one power went off and everybody had to use candle lights. It used to happen many times, so there was no worry to look for candles. It was thundering and stormy, people just in at one place where they could hardly see anything.

In those days people worked very hard and earned quite a lot of money. At that time the average wage of a village worker was about 50p to £5.00 a week, it was much in those days.

My famiily was a very poor family who tried to save money and tried getting out of that country but unfortunately nobody could manage this. My parents' earnings were about the average but as the family was very big the money ran out like water from a tap. Nobody could help us although everyone in the village tried.

After a few years we came to Bradford, which was a good place to live and work. My parents decided to go into business making Ladies and Gents leather wear. It took some time finding a suitable place. After a year we found a place in Greenford on one west side of London. It was a factory which was closing down. About five shops could be made from the place. My parents' business progressed very well. All our orders came from Manchester, Leeds, Germany and Switzerland. At that time I must be exactly fourteen years old. My sister thirteen and my younger brother ten.

I remember when, we had stayed at our aunt's house in Bradford, she asked my parents for the money for when we stayed at her place

until we found our own house. I remember when she said:
"I gave you life and a place to live in. Otherwise, I think by now, you should be begging on the streets, you're very lucky to have an aunt like me."
My parents did not say anything but gave her the money as soon as we left. My parents didn't want any trouble or to start rumours around the world. It surely was a time to remember what people were like.

When my aunt heard that our business is progressing well she came to meet my parents at the work place. She started saying,
"Oh what a lovely place, oh you're getting on well aren't you, congratulations!" My parents didn't say a word. She went around looking at the place and touching the garments.My mother then asked her, "Would you like a cup of tea?" "Oh how kind, but don't bother, I'd be going soon." She said in a most curious way.

My parents asked her for dinner on the same evening. She not only stayed in that evening but had stayed at our house for exactly seven weeks. My parents were telling her the things which she had told about my parents. She denied everything. She said:— "I didn't say a word like that, how could you say a thing like that to me." I remember all those things or what you call NONSENSE! I know how my parents felt in their hearts. I know what sort of things she and not only she but other relatives too who said so many things like:— "Look they can't afford a house or a shop." "God help them they don't know what to do, just look at the children's clothes how thin they look." "We don't want to go down their house, where you can't sit in comfort." "We wonder what they are going to do by the time the children grow up. How are they going to get their daughters married with what a load of rubbish!"

My family and I know what has been done with our lives, and our future which is getting better and better by the help of Allah the almighty one only one but Allah!

You see people, what I mean by people is everyone brother, sister, relative, friend they all love you when you have money, they will all respect you when? ... When you are rich with money, houses, bungalows, cars, etc.

My parents have been through this miserable life but what matters to the world is MONEY. Whoever has money also has respect but whoever has not are beggars.

We came to understand that a sister is a sister when you have money, this problem can arise between any relationship no matter if it's a father and son or a husband and a wife or a mother and daughter no matter who. They will be with you if you love them but with what? MONEY.

We have been to Pakistan, India and parts of Kashmir. Our life is much more enjoyable than before. People are with us now but I don't know for how long maybe until we go poor again. Who's saying we're rich. We're not rich not yet, people are gradually coming forward because they know they could get something to eat from us or to wear.

Our life now is much better we're not poor or rich we're what you would call okay, but people don't believe that they all say that we're rich mind you we're not!

JASMIN

۔ جب آپ مالدار ہونگے ۔ بیمہ کار، بینکاں آپ کے پاس ہوگا ۔
بہرے دالدین زندگی کی ان مہینوں اور مشکلات سے گزرے ہیں مگر اپنا
ذہن یہی بنا جاتی ہے ۔ ایسے پیسے ہی سروکار ہے ۔ جس کے پاس دولت
ہے اسکے پاس عزت ہے مجی ہے اور جس کے پاس دولت نہیں وہ فقیر ہے ۔
ہم اس نتیجے پر پہنچے ہیں کہ جہں تو وقت تک ہمارے پاس جب تک آپ کے
پاس پیسہ ہے ۔ اس قسم کی بریتانی کی مجی دفعتی کی اولاد تی لکتی ہے ۔
چاہے باپ ہو بیٹا ہو شوہر ہو بیوی ہو ماں ہو بیٹی ہو چاہے جو ہو
یہ سب آپ کے ساتھ ہیں گے اور آپ سے پیار کریں گے مگر پیسے کے ساتھ
ہم لگ ہندوستان پاکستان اور کشمیر کے سبھی حصوں میں کے دیکھے ۔ ہماری زندگی
اب پہلے سے کہیں زیادہ پر لطف ہے ۔ لوگوں کی نظر عنایت ہم پر ہے مگر یہ
پتہ نہیں کہ تک شاید جب تک جب تک ہم دبادہ غریب ہوں کن کہرا
ہے کہ ہم ایبربیں؟ ہم ایبربیں ہیں ابھی ہیں ۔ لگ آہستہ آہستہ ہماری لڑن بولیو
بہریں کیونکہ اپنی پتہ ہے کہ اپنی ہمارے پاس سے روٹی کپڑا اللہ جائگا؟ ۔

ہماری زندگی بہت بہتر ہے ۔ ہم نہ ایبربیں نہ غریب ۔ مکملت ہیں اور وسط درجے کے
نگر رنگ یقین نہی ملنتی امیکتہ ہیں کہ ہم ایبربیں ۔ جواد ہم امیربیں ۔
بہرحال اب مجھے یہ کہانی ختم کرنی چاہیے اِ کہ اس ایسے کے ساتھ کہ ماما نانران اور
دوسرے نانران بہی نشتی دیں ۔ اور کسی کو بھی کسی طرح کی نفرت کا سامنا
کرنا پڑے ۔ ہماری دعا ہے کہ اللہ ا ایہین سہمائنی کہ کرزدرمت ہون
دے ۔ اپنی دنیا کی لئے مشکینوں کا سامنا اور سبرداشت ہونے کی ہمت دے ۔ اور
مستقبل میں اُن والی نئی نسلوں کی ذہنیت میں بہادری بھنا ہے کہ نہ بھی زندگی
ہی مشکینوں کا سامنا کرنے کے لئل ہوں ۔

یاسمین

۔ مجھے بری طرح ان سے بڑ بچھا

"کہ کیا آپ بانے بیبا پنر کریں گی؟"

بڑے مہربان مگر ۔ بیٹے دیں اتنی ذحمت نہ کریں میں بس بس بات
ہی والی ہوں انہوں نے بڑے تجسس کے انداز میں کہا ۔

میرے دل الدین نے ان سے دانت کے مسکانے کے لئے دعوت دی وہ صرف
اسی دانت ہیں بلکہ لوے سات ہفتے ہمارے گھر دیں ۔ میرے دل الدین
نے انہیں وہ تمام باتیں یاد دلائیں و وہ پہلے کہا کہنے نہی مگر انہوں نے ہر
بات کا انکار کر دیا اور کہا ۔

'میں نے اسی طرح کا ایک لفظ بھی تم سے نہی کہا یہ تم لوگ کس طرح کی
باتیں کرتے ہو ۔

مجھے اس وقت کی ہر بک اس طرح یاد ہے ۔ اور یہ بھی پتہ ہے کہ میرے
دل الدین کے دل پر اس وقت کیا گزری تھی ۔ مجھے معلوم ہے کہ اس قسم کی
باتیں نہ صرف انہوں بلکہ ہمارے اور رشتے داروں نے صحاب کی نہی جیسے ۔
دیکھو نہ یہ مکان یا دکان تک ہیں فرید کیلے' فرا ہی ان کی مدد کرے'
ذرا ان کے بچوں کے کپڑے نہ دیکھو ہم ان کے گھر باہر کیا کریں
اور ام سے سیدھا تک نہ سکتے ہیں ہیں ۔ بہنے ہیں یہ لوگ اس وقت
کیا کریں گے جب ان کے بچے ہوں گے۔ آخر یہ کس طرح اپنی لڑکیوں
کی شادیاں کریں گے ۔

مجھے اور میرے خاندان کی یہ معلوم ہے کہ ہم سب پر کیا وقت پڑا
ہے اور ہم نے زندگی میں ایسے دن دیکھے ہیں ۔ اور ہمارا مستقبل ہو دن
بہن پنر ہوتا جا رہا ہے وہ طرف اور صرف اللہ کی مہربانی سے ۔
آپ نے دیکھا لگے لگتے میری مراد کہ بھی مہائی بہن رشتہ دار
دست و اصحاب یہ سب آپ سے پیار کریں گے آپ کی غزت کریں گے کب؟

۔ایک ابھی بگڈ ثابت ہوئی؟ ۔ میرے والدین نے چوراہے کے کارڈ بورڈ کا ارادہ کیا۔ جس نے مناسب کی بگڈ کی تلاشی میں کچھ دن لیا۔

ایک سال بعد ہمیں لندن کے مغربی علاقے بریٹ فورڈ میں بگڈ مل گئی ۔ یہ ایک بیکری تھی ۔ و کی بند ہونے جا رہی تھی اور اسی بگڈ پر تقریباً بائیں دکانیں بن سکتی تھیں ۔

میرے والدین کے کارڈ بورڈ نے خوب ترقی کی ۔ مانچسٹر، لیڈز، برمنگھم اور سوئٹزرلینڈ سے ہمارے پاس آرڈر آنے لگے ۔ اس وقت میں ۱۳ سال کی عمر میں تھی ۱۲ سال کی اور برا بھائی ۱۰ سال کا تھا۔

مجھے یاد ہے جب ہم بریٹ فورڈ میں اپنی انکل کے گھر میں رہتے تھے اور جب تک ہمیں اپنا گھر نہیں مل گیا انہوں نے ہم سے اپنے بیان کرنے کے پیسے مانگے ۔

مجھے یاد ہے جب انہوں نے کہا ۔

میں نے تمہیں زندگی دی اور رہنے کے لئے بگڈ ۔ ورنہ اس وقت تک تم کہیں بلٹ پر بھیک مانگ رہے ہوتے ۔ تم لوگ بڑے خوش قسمت ہو کہ نہیں میری بہی انٹی لی ۔

میرے والدین نے ان سے سبجی نہیں کہا اور سکھہ چھوڑنے ہی اپنی بیٹی دے دی۔ کیونک وہ کسی مصیبت میں نہیں پڑنا چاہتے تھے ۔ یہ یاد دیکھنے کا وقت تھا کہ لگ کیسے پیسے ہونے ہیں ۔

جب میری انٹی کی ہمارے کارڈ بورڈ کی ترقی کی قبر ملی تو وہ ہم سے ملنے آئیں اور اس طرح شروع ہو گئیں ۔

اے یہ تو بڑی پیاری بگڈ ہے ۔ تم لگ کتنی ترقی کر رہے ہو ۔ مبارک ہو ۔ میرے والدین نے ان سے ایک لفظ نہیں کہا اور وہ اِدھر اُدھر دیکھنے لگیں ۔ برتنوں کی چھوٹی چھیلی دیں ۔

پیسوں کی متوالی دنیا

یہ ۱۹۷۰ کی بات ہے جب میں بہت چھوٹی تھی۔ ۱۱-۱۰ سال کی
بچی۔ میں پاکستان میں تھی اور ایک بہت ہی چھوٹی سی چوبیری میں
رہتی تھی۔ جی کی دولادیں اتنی فٹ مال نہیں کہ محسوس ہوتا غالبی
گر پردیس کی ۔ اس کی جہت ایسی تھی کہ جب کبھی طونان آتا تو
اس کے چھوٹے چھوٹے ٹکڑے کھم اور اڑ کر دوسروں کے سروں پر گرا
کرتے تھے ۔

میں سوچا کرتی تھی کہ کس طرح میرے دالدین ایسی جگہ رہ رہے ہیں۔
اور اکثر بجلی نہیں ہو جاتے تو ہر آدمی کو موم بتی استعمال کرنی پڑتی تھی۔
اور ایسا اکثر ہو بینتس ہوا کرتا تھا اس لیے کوئ موم بتی تلاشی کرنے کی
زحمت ہی نہیں کراتا کرتا تھا غظ پختا۔ جب آخر بھی طونان یا سمان ہا ہوتا تھا
تو تگ کہاں کے تہاں نہ جاتے تھے۔ اس زمانے میں لوگ سخت محنت
کرتے اور لنجمے فاضے بیسے کما لیتے تھے۔ گاڈن میں کام کرنے دالوں کی تنخواہ
کا اوسط ۵۰ پیسے سے لیکر ۲ ڈنر فی ہفتہ تک تھا۔ وہ اس وقت کے لحاظ سے کافی
تھا۔

میرا تعلق ایک غریب خاندان سے تھا جی نے پیسے بچلنے اور وطن سے
باہر مانگنے بڑی کوشنی کی گر ہر قسمی سے کوئ بھی ایسا کرنے میں
کامیاب نہیں ہوا۔ میرے دالدین کی آمدنی بھی اوسط کے حساب سے تھی
گر بڑا خاندان ہونے کی وجہ سے بیسا اسی طرح بہنا تھا جی طرح ل
سے پانی۔ گاڈن دالوں نے جماری مود کرنے کی بڑی کوشنی کی گر کوئ
بھی کامیاب نہیں ہوا۔

کچھ دنوں بعد ہم بریڈ فورڈ آپ کے ۔۔۔ کس دینے اور کام کرنے کے لحاظ سے

WHEN YOU DON'T FEEL LIKE A FOREIGNER

It is never easy being a foreigner in a country; it is even more difficult when you don't feel like a foreigner.

I am an Asian girl, originally from India, though I was born here in England 18 years ago. I live in relative comfort in an exceptionally nice area of the town, with all the amenities and many of the luxuries at my disposal. I enjoy my life here and would find it difficult to imagine living in another country.

I think people in all spheres of live are bound to experience prejudice at one time or another, be it for their race, colour or creed but perhaps we are subject to prejudice in all these areas. I have found that there are two main types of prejudice, the kind that is expressed in loud explicit and often violent tones, the other a more subtle though no less expressive type. The former I do not experience directly very often and as yet never in its violent form. It is intimidating to have to walk past a group of young 'skinheads' and suffer being called names such as 'smelly paki' or 'chocolate drop' or have to cross the road to avoid a group of older 'skinheads'. I believe these human beings who look and sound as they do are as much a pest to English people as they are to us Asians.

The second form of prejudice is the type I encounter with my good friends. My best friends are all English and white. Phraseslike 'I don't think of you as being an Indian, I mean you don't smell of curry or speak with an Indian accent'. Often they astonish me in their naivety of thinking that all Indians are like that. Another interesting example of prejudice amongst friends is a conversation I had with a boy I was going out with at the time. He simply adored me and I him but he could not accept my being superior to him in any way. We were discussing our 'O' level results and although he did not do as well as me he insisted that had he worked harder or even worked at all he would have done better than me. I thought at first that this was because I was a girl, but from later conversations I realised that it was because I was an Indian girl.

Parental care, to all appearances, is much more protective and thus restrictive in Indian homes than in English ones. From my own experience I find it extremely annoying especially since my friends are not treated in the same way. My parents insist on knowing where I am when I go out, though not necessarily who I am with, what time I will be home and how I am getting home. Whereas my friends are allowed to walk home after a party, although they must tell their parents at what time they will be home. Personally I find this an overprotective part of my parents' nature, but of course, having spoken to many other Indian girls in my college this constitutes complete freedom in comparison to them. Naturally since most of us are influenced to a high degree by the views of our parents, maybe many of my own ideas are simply extensions of those of my parents and often my own ideas are in conflict with those of my friends.

Marriage of course is a major topic of conversation for girls of my age, since hopefully, within the next few years we all hope to be married. My friends find my marriage arrangements interesting because they are never sure whether or not a marriage is to be arranged for me. My views on this subject have changed over the years. Until a few years ago I felt arranged marriages to be very unromantic and I couldn't understand how couples could be content with this arrangement. I then began speaking to girls who considered an arranged marriage to be acceptable, in some cases even desirable. Having increased in years and experience my views have been somewhat tempered. I now believe that, from reading recent statistics, 'love' marriages are not more successful than arranged marriages; however, I feel that it is the freedom of choice in a 'love' marriage that makes me covet one. I feel that I should have a complete choice in the man with whom I am to spend the rest of my life with, the chance to make up my own mind about the person I could be happy with, the freedom to decide my future be it right or the wrong choice.

Religion is a subject which many of us have no choice about. If one is born into Hindu, Muslim or Christian households, one is compelled to live by the rules and traditions dictated by that religion. Personally I do not believe that religion is in any way a wonderful thing. Blind faith in anything is shortsighted but following traditions when they are not your true beliefs is perhaps worse.

I am an Indian girl in England and the conflicts this causes are sometimes quite frightening but I would rather live in England with all the faults than anywhere else.

RITA

A CITIZEN OF THE WORLD

I was born in Calcutta, my father is English and my mother Indian. I now, after much world—trotting, am living and working in London.

Coming from a background like this one has to come to terms with and try to understand one's own identity at an early age. "Where do you feel you belong" is a question you get used to hearing. The answer grows as you do. Until I was 15 I belonged to where my parents lived and that included Canada. Then I went to boarding school in England and home was only a holiday home. From then till I went back to Delhi three years later to live with my parents for a year, I was an independent spirit. Because of this I find that I can put down roots wherever I happen to be and call that place home. I suppose I think of myself as a citizen of the world. India pulls me because of memories of childhood, old friends, familiar places, family and the excitement of there being so much undiscovered in my own motherland. England too, has given me many friends, most of my education and an independence which India denied me. Both countries have their own advantages and disadvantages.

However, my mother is a Christian Indian (from Goa, originally), and so has herself been brought up divorced from Indian culture and educated with a western bias. Because of this I feel less Indian than friends of mine with the same mixed parentage, but with a Muslim mother. I think this is important, because I feel that the biggest difference between east and west is the difference of religion. In my case, it was more a case of "westernised east" meets "west", than east meets west. India's culture is bound by religion and its codes of behaviour and social codes are derived from its religion. In England this is not so.

My feelings for India are very strong because there is so much about this land that I have not yet learnt. I hope to go back to live in India one day. However, if I went back I would expect to do things my own way and would probably be living there as a foreigner and not as an Indian, which would be too far removed from the beliefs that I hold. There are many things about India that I cannot agree with—

the rules and regulations about young people and the restraints placed on them which cause unnatural hang—ups between boys and girls, frustrations and unpleasantness, which I have experienced, myself.

Indians look at me with some amazement and also amusement. In Delhi my relatives are slightly put—off by my self—confidence and strong beliefs. They are disturbed that my parents have "let me go". My own mother is disappointed (to say the least) that family feeling did not keep me in Delhi permanently. However western an education she had, she cannot accept that a daughter of hers followed her heart—and head—back to London, rather than staying in the relative safety of "home". I am considered something of an oddity.

Even Indian relatives who have travelled abroad are somewhat mystified. For them England is a different England to the one I inhabit. Cousins of my own age—or younger—are very bad at concealing their jealousy and are frankly admiring of my sisters and I. Perhaps we are achieving the independence they want and without *TOO* much struggle.

In England at school and then at my secretarial college, there was an equivalent lack of comprehension. This, though, was caused by lack of knowledge. I think this has been put right somewhat by last year's concentration on India in the Festival. An English view of India until then had been somewhat limited. Limited to books about the Raj (Paul Scott, etc.) and stories told by old India hands.

A lot of the racial problems, I feel, were caused by the dearth of information—the right kind of relevant information. Unfortunately, because of this evidence of lack of information, Asians in London and Indians at home felt a resentment towards England and towards this attitude. With this resentment built up it will take a lot of understanding on both sides to make relations between the 2 countries more accepting. It will take time, though I hope things will improve more rapidly. Hopefully, with more younger English people travelling further and further away from home and becoming more aware of the rest of the world—especially the east—this will happen in my generation. I sincerely hope so.

ANN ROHINI

INDIANS IN ANOTHER COUNTRY

Firstly, I'd rather say Indian than Asian, because Asia is a large continent with numerous cultures and traditions, thus the label "Asian" cannot identify an individual like me. "Indian" is better, but knowing that my origins are from Gujarat, and that I am a Hindu may help to characterize me more specifically.

You have asked me how I feel being an Indian within the family, and in a British society. Many researchers like to emphasize a "culture conflict" between the generations in an Asian community. But I have never felt a strong conflict between the two cultures. I feel that I have developed to be able to adapt and accommodate to the two cultures on most occasions.

I say on most occasions, because there have been a few times when I have felt my "Asian" identity rather than my "personal" identity stand out. For example, at University when some of my friends have got drunk, and I have not because for me it is very disrespectable for an Indian girl to get drunk—there has been a conflict where I have had to make a decision upon how to behave. By the way, I'd rather be respectable—as I feel is respectable.

Another area of conflict occurs for many Indian girls, when their friends have boyfriends. I have never had a deep relationship with a person of the opposite sex. This is my own choice. From a very young age (15 years) I have known boys, but I have always consciously not become too involved, mainly because none has been the right person so far—someone whom I would like to marry. I cannot see the point of having a fun relationship. I have many male friends, my family know who they are, and I can invite them home. I get as much out of these friendships without the need for deeper relationships.

My nuclear family consists of my three sisters, mother and father. We have an extremely large extended family which has its advantages and disadvantages. For example, where the parents' behaviour is governed by relatives than by their own opinions; then I feel that this is wrong. But a large family can give security, company and closeness of people; and keep the good nature of caring which is essential in a society that is becoming more inhumane of the care of elderly.

My parents have been living here in London for about 25 years. I would describe ours as a middle–class family. Our family is not anglicised. I can communicate in Gujarati. My mother wears a sari always and her English is not good—she understands English but finds it difficult to speak in that language. I wear saris on special occasions that way it can still be a novelty. I was born in London, but have visited India at 14 years for 6 weeks. In my home, we follow many of the Indian traditions, e.g. food, clothes and marriage. Our family is not very religious though my father only knows the basics of the Hindu religion as I do. My mother follows the religion in that she "fasts" sometimes, and will have a "diva". The reason why I am not religious is because my family have never encouraged me to be, and also I do not agree with following a religion blindly without getting any meaning from it.

When "people" speak of arranged marriages, this is the example that they use as an area of culture conflict between the generations of an Asian society. I feel that conflict in this area is emphasised more than it exists. I have done a questionnaire project and found (amongst many other things) that more people are "for" than "against" marriages. What happens is that all bad news makes the media. The media and many others who study Asian youths speak as if they are bound to reject their culture if brought up in another country. But they forget that Asian individuals live within a family unit which is influential in the development of any individual. A person spends a lot of their life time with the family—especially if he/she is Indian.

I feel that being able to "communicate" with my father has enabled me to adapt ideas suited to both an Indian and a British society— especially on ideas related to arranged marriages like most other Indian girls, when I was 16 years, I decided I wasn't going to have an arranged marriage. How could I marry someone I didn't know? Luckily for me, I have been able to have my questions answered through communication, and the exchange of ideas with older and equally aged persons to me. I feel that communication is essential if young people are to adopt the ideas of their elder generation. This is because there are no other people in the British society, that they can speak to, or that can understand the intricacies of the Indian culture. One thing that young people need to understand is that their parents were brought up in a society where arranged marriage was the only type they knew about. Thus, perhaps nobody spoke to them about arranged marriages; and this could make it difficult for them to speak on them. Therefore, young people should try to initiate a conversation.

I don't think parents should be blamed. Instead, they should be helped. I do not see myself as lucky to have understanding parents. It is all to do with forming a communicative relationship, actively on the part of me where some subjects are concerned. For a good relationship, there needs to be co−operation on both sides. People should remember that, like most other things, an arranged marriage is not all bad, nor all good. Arranged marriages are not primitive compared to love marriages. There are pros and cons for both. I have spoken of arranged marriages as I know—there is no single definition of an arranged marriage.

Also, an arranged marriage is multi−dimensional. Different castes and sub-castes practise different marriage traditions. Changes have occurred in marriage practices over the years that have made "arranged" ones more acceptable. Thus, there does not have to be complete abolition. There is no clear right or wrong answer.

We, as Indians in another country, are in the advantageous situation of being able to perceive both cultures. We should use this to our benefit by taking in all the goodness from both worlds.

I personally have not felt a "culture conflict". I have adapted. I have made decisions from all the information and thinking of ideas. Arranged marriages cannot be stereotyped, nor can Indian parents, and nor can young Indian people. To obtain a fair view, not only should studies be done using Indian boys and girls; but also parents. They should be given a fair chance to be subjects.

SHILA PATEL

'પરાયા દેશમાં ભારતીય જનો.'   શીલા.

સૌ પ્રથમ હું પોતાને એશિયન કરતા ભારતીય ગણાવું કારણ કે એશિયા ખંડ ખૂબ વિશાળ અને વિવિધ સંસ્કૃતિ તથા રૂઢિઓથી ભરપૂર છે. તેથી મારા જેવી વ્યક્તિની ઓળખ માટે 'એશિયન' લેબલ આપવું મને યોગ્ય લાગતું નથી. હું એક ભારતીય વ્યક્તિ છું. મારું મૂળ વતન ગુજરાત છે તથા હું હિંદુ ધર્મમાં શ્રદ્ધા ધરાવું છું. આ બાબતો મારા વ્યક્તિત્વને જરા વધુ સ્પષ્ટ રીતે પ્રગટ કરે છે.

એક ભારતીય વ્યક્તિ તરીકે મારા કુટુંબ વિશે તથા અંગ્રેજ સમાજ પ્રત્યે મારા શું વિચારો છે એ વિશે તમે મને પ્રશ્ન કર્યો છે. ઘણા લોકોએ આ બાબતને રીસર્ચ કરી છે તેઓ આ સમસ્યાને 'ભારતીય સમાજમાં સંસ્કૃતિનો સંઘર્ષ' એ શીર્ષક આપે છે. પરંતુ આ બે સંસ્કૃતિઓ વચ્ચેનો આવો કૈક સંઘર્ષ મેં પોતે આજ સુધી અનુભવ્યો નથી. મારા ધારવા પ્રમાણે ઘણા ખરા પ્રસંગોએ આ બંને સંસ્કૃતિઓનું સામ્યપણ આણવા માટે અને બંનેને અનુકૂળ થવા માટે મેં પોતાને પ્રબળ કરી છે.

મારા જીવનમાં ઘણા એવા પ્રસંગો આવ્યા છે જેમાં મારી વ્યક્તિગત 'ભારતીય' ઓળખ કરતા 'એશિયન' ઓળખ આગળ તરી આવે છે. દાખલા તરીકે યુનિવર્સિટીમાં મારા આશીઆરો દારૂ પીએ છે પરંતુ એક ભારતીય નારી માટે એ ખૂબ નામોશીભર્યું કહેવાય તેથી દારૂ પીવાની બાબતને હું મારા મિત્રોને સહકાર આપતી નથી. જો કે આવા પ્રસંગે મારે કેવો વ્યવહાર કરવો જોઈએ એ વિશે મારા મનમાં અનેક સંઘર્ષ થાય છે પણ હું પોતાને માનનીય રાખવા પ્રયત્ન કરું છું.

ઘણી ભારતીય છોકરીઓ પોતાના જીવનમાં સંઘર્ષ અનુભવે છે જ્યારે એમની સહેલીઓને પુરુષ મિત્રો જોય છે. મારા જીવનમાં મારી સ્વેચ્છાથી મેં કોઈપણ પુરુષ મિત્ર સાથે ગાઢી મૈત્રી આજ સુધી રાખી નથી. પંદર વર્ષની નાની ઉંમરથી જ હું ઘણા યુવાન છોકરાઓના સંપર્કમાં આવું છું. હું એમને ઓળખું છું પરંતુ કોઈની પણ સાથે ધાર્મિક સંબંધ મેં જાળી-જોઈને રાખ્યો નથી. આ બધા પુરુષમિત્રોમાંથી કોઈપણ મને મારે લાયક (લગ્ન કરવા માટે) લાગ્યું નથી. માત્ર મજા માણવાના હેતુથી જ કોઈની સાથે ગાઢ સંબંધ રાખવો એ મને યોગ્ય લાગતું નથી. મારા બધા મિત્રોને મારા કુટુંબીજનો મારી રીતે ઓળખાને છે. જ્યારે પણ ઈચ્છા થાય ત્યારે મારા કુટુંબીજનોના વિરોધ વગર હું મારા પુરુષ મિત્રોને મારે ઘેર આમંત્રણ આપી શકું છું. વધુ નિકટ આવ્યા વગર પણ હું આવી સામાન્ય મૈત્રીનો લાભ ઉઠાવી શકું છું.

મારા કુટુંબમાં મારા માતાપિતા તથા નાના બહેનો છે પરંતુ સગા સ્નેહીઓ સાથે અમારું આખું પરિવાર ખૂબ વિશાળ છે.

આ પ્રકારના વિશાળ પરિવાર બંધાવાના ફાયદા અને સંયુક્તતા બંને છે. દાખલા તરીકે ઘણા સંજોગોમાં માબાપ પોતાની ઇચ્છા પ્રમાણે નિર્ણય લઈ શકતા નથી. પરિવારના અન્ય સભ્યોના વિચારો અને મન્તવ્યોને ધ્યાનમાં રાખીને પછી નિર્ણય લેવાય છે. આ બાબત મને યોગ્ય લાગતી નથી. પરંતુ મારા પરિવારનો એક ફાયદો એ છે કે એમાં એકબીજની હૂંફની લિજ્જત અને પરંપરા સંરક્ષણની ભાવના હંમેશા જળવાય રહે છે. આજના સમાજમાં વૃદ્ધ વડીલવર્ગની સારસંભાળ પ્રત્યે જે બાપરવાઈ વધતી જાય છે એ મારા કુટુંબની ફૂંગમાં આપોઆપ જળવાય જાય છે.

મારા માતાપિતા લગભગ પચ્ચીસ વર્ષોથી આ દેશમાં રહે છે. અમારૂં કુટુંબ મધ્યમ વર્ગનું કહી શકાય. અમારા કુટુંબમાં અંગ્રેજ પદ્ધતિ અપનાવાઈ નથી. હું પોતે ગુજરાતી ભાષામાં એકબીજા સાથે વાતચીત કરી શકું છું. મારી બા હંમેશા સાડી પહેરે છે. એને અંગ્રેજી ભાષા બરાબર આવડતી નથી. એ અંગ્રેજી સમજ શકે છે પણ પણ બરાબર બોલી શકતા નથી. કેટલાક પ્રસંગોમાં હું પણ સાડી પહેરું છું કારણ કે એ મને એક જાતની નોવેલ્ટી લાગે છે.

મારો જન્મ લંડનમાં થયો હતો. ૧૪ વર્ષની ઉંમરે હું છ અઠવાડિયા માટે ભારત ફરવા માટે ગઈ હતી. ખોરાક, પોષાક તથા લગ્નવિધિ જેવી બાબતોમાં અમારા કુટુંબમાં ભારતના હિંદુ રીતરિવાજોની ખૂબ અસર હોય છે. અમે ખૂબ ધાર્મિક વૃત્તિના નથી. હું અને મારા પિતાજી હિંદુ ધર્મના મૂળ સિદ્ધાંતોથી જાણકાર છીએ. મારી બા હિંદુ ધર્મમાં વધારે શ્રદ્ધા ધરાવે છે. ઘણીવાર ઉપવાસ કરે છે. દીવો કરી ભજવવાની રૂઢ કરે છે. મારા વડીલોએ મને ધાર્મિક બનવાનો ઉત્સાહ આપ્યો નથી તેથી મારૂં વલણ બહુ ધાર્મિક નથી. ધર્મનો ગૂઢ અર્થ સમજ્યા વગર ધર્મને અંધશ્રદ્ધાથી પાળવો એ મને યોગ્ય લાગતું નથી.

જ્યારે લોકો વડીલોની સંમતિથી ગોઠવાયેલ લગ્ન (Arranged Marraige) વિષે ચર્ચા કરે છે ત્યારે મોટા ભાગે એશિયન સમાજની પેઢીઓના સંસ્કૃતિ સંઘર્ષનો ઉલ્લેખ વિશેષ કરે છે. આ બાબતનું મહત્વ છે એના કરતાં વધારે પડતું વધારવામાં આવે છે. મેં આ વિષય પર પ્રશ્નાવલિઓ તૈયાર કરીને જે માહિતી મેળવી છે એના પરથી સાબિત થાય છે કે ઘણી મોટી સંખ્યામાં લોકો આ પ્રકારના ગોઠવણીના લગ્નોમાં સંમતિ ધરાવે છે. સામાન્ય રીતે એવું બને છે કે કોઈપણ બાબતમાં કંઈ અનિષ્ટ તત્વ હોય છે એનો પ્રચાર પ્રેસ મારફતે વધુ થાય છે.

પરદેશમાં ઉછરતા યુવાનો વિષે રીસર્ચ કરનાર પત્રકારો વગેરેનું એવું મન્તવ્ય હોય છે કે આવા પરદેશી યુવાનોએ આ દેશમાં રહેતા પોતાની મૂળ સંસ્કૃતિનો ત્યાગ કરવો જ પડે છે. પરંતુ આ રીસર્ચ કરનારાઓ એ ભૂલી જતા લાગે છે કે

કુટુંબમાં બીજાઓની સાથે રહેવાથી વ્યક્તિના જીવન વિકાસ પર એની ઘણી અસર થાય છે. ઈંડિયન છોકરો કે છોકરી પોતાના જીવનનો ઘણો બધો સમય પોતાના કુટુંબ સાથે ગુજારે છે.

મારા પિતાજી સાથે વિચારોની આપલે કરવાની મને સારી તક મળી છે. એને પરિણામે ભારતીય અને અંગ્રેજ આ બંને સમાજોના યોગ્ય આદર્શો અપનાવવા માટે હું સમર્થ બની શકી છું.

દા.ત. વડીલોની સંમતિથી ગોઠવાયેલ લગ્ન વિષેના આદર્શો. જ્યારે હું ૧૬ વર્ષની હતી ત્યારે મેં પાકો નિર્ણય કર્યો હતો કે હું આ પ્રકારના લગ્ન કરવાની નથી. જે વ્યક્તિને હું ઓળખતી નથી, જાણતી નથી એની સાથે લગ્ન કેવી રીતે થઈ શકે? સદ્ભાગ્યે મારા મનની આવી મૂંઝવણોના સંતોષકારક જવાબો હું મારા વડીલો મારફતે મેળવી શકું છું. વડીલો ઉપરાંત મારી પોતાની ઉંમરની વ્યક્તિઓ સાથે પણ હું વિચારોની આપલે કરી શકું છું. આજના યુવાન વર્ગે જો વડીલ પેઢીઓના વિચારો અપનાવવા હોય તો પરસ્પર વિચારોની આપલે કરવી એ અનિવાર્ય છે. કારણકે અંગ્રેજ સમાજમાં એવા કોઈ લોકો નથી કે જેઓ ઇંડિયન સંસ્કૃતિનું મહત્ત્વ બરાબર સમજી શકે અને આવા લોકો સાથે એશિયન યુવાનો વિચારોની આપલે કરી શકે એ શક્ય નથી. અને ભાવત યુવાનવર્ગે ધ્યાનમાં રાખવાની છે કે એમના માબાપો એવા સમાજમાં ઉછરેલા છે જેમાં આ પ્રકારના વડીલોની સંમતિથી ગોઠવાયેલ લગ્ન જ થઈ શકતા. તેથી મારા ધારવા પ્રમાણે માબાપોને દોષ દેવા કરતા મદદરૂપ થવું એ વધુ ઈચ્છવાયોગ્ય છે.

ગોઠવણીના લગ્નના પણ બે પાસા છે. એ સંપૂર્ણ દોષ-રહિત છે કે દોષયુક્ત છે એવું નથી. એના ફાયદા અને ગેરફાયદા બંને છે. આ પ્રકારના લગ્નના વિવિધ પાસા છે. વિવિધ શાસ્ત્રીઓ લગ્નની જુદી જુદી પ્રથાઓ ધરાવે છે. વર્ષોના વહાણા સાથે લગ્નપ્રથાઓ બદલાતી ગઈ છે. પરિણામે આ પ્રકારના લગ્ન આજે વધારે માન્ય થતા જાય છે તેથી મારા મતે આ પ્રકારના લગ્નોની સંપૂર્ણ ખામી ન થવી જોઈએ.

અમે ઇંડિયન લોકો પરદેશમાં રહીને ઇંડિયન અને અંગ્રેજ બંને સમાજની સંસ્કૃતિઓનું સંકલન કરી શકીને છીએ તેથી બંને દેશોનું જે કાંઈ સારું છે તેનો ઉપયોગ આપણા લાભાર્થે થવો જોઈએ.

મેં પોતે કોઈ જાતનો સાંસ્કૃતિક સંઘર્ષ અનુભવ્યો નથી. હું પરિસ્થિતિને અનુકૂળ થઈ શકી છું. મારા કેટલાક આદર્શો અને મેળવેલી માહિતીને આધારે હું પોતે નિર્ણય લઈ શકું છું. આપણા વિવાહનો સમતોલ અર્થ મેળવવા માટે માત્ર ઇંડિયન છોકરા-છોકરીઓને જ નહિ પણ માબાપોને પણ રીસર્ચમાં શામેલ કરવા જોઈએ.

વધારાની માહિતી:-

વડીલોની સંમતિથી ગોઠવાયેલ લગ્નપ્રથાની કોઈ અને ખાસ પરિભાષા નથી. અને વિષેની મને જેટલી માહિતી છે અને આધારે મેં આ પ્રથા સમજાવવા પ્રયત્ન કર્યો છે.

મારા વિચારોમાં સમજ ધરાવનાર મારા માતાપિતા છે તેથી કદી હું પોતાને ભાગ્યશાળી સમજતી નથી. કેટલીક પરિસ્થિતિમાં મારે પોતાને એમની સાથે મતભેદનો સંબંધ કેળવવો પડે છે. બંને પક્ષે સહકાર હોવો અને સારા સંબંધ માટે ખૂબ જરૂરી છે.

દીવા - માટીનું કે બીજા કોઈ ધાતુનું કોડિયું - જેમાં (ઘી) તેલ મૂકી રૂ ની વાટ કરી સળગાવીને દેવ કે દેવીની મૂર્તિ સામે મૂકીને પૂજા કરવા માટે વપરાય છે.

STILL THAT RACIST ATTITUDE

Last 11 years I am in London with my husband—our little girl is only 6 years. Recently I went to Dacca, my home with my daughter. As she is getting interested about our family, our language, dance and music we thought it will be nice and right time to take her now—for our family it was great joy to meet her. Also both of us think it is our duty to take our daughter to her grandparents. Their blessings and happiness is something which we value more than anything in this world. As a youngest in the family—I find this separation from my family very painful. Though I have got a very loving and considerate husband, also a comfortable home. It will sound silly to many of my English and European friends, still after so many years, I miss my parents, brothers and sisters, aunts so much. Specially when we go somewhere nice wish my family were with me. So when I look at this country's family life I feel very strange and sad. Simply they don't know what they are missing and the love, affection, care and protection I was surrounded by my parents, brother, sisters—now by my husband—the warmth and the peaceful secure feeling inside me is wonderful.

I think I **am** very lucky—though our marriage was arranged—it really work out extremely well. After coming here my husband has got his Ph.D. in Chemistry. He came here with job voucher—not only the job but to do the Ph.D. was also our main reason to come in this country. It is shame and funny still today we value British degree. Many of my friends who could not or can't gain British degree, they feel great deal of shame and failure inside them. It does not matter how much money or how expensive house or car he got—we have got great weakness and respect for British education. We have made many friends—many of them English and very nice.

I used to wonder why there is all this talk about racist society? It was in 1978, we were living near Well St., E9, in an old block of flats. We were the only Asian family. Lali was 8 months old. My neighbours were very friendly and kind to our daughter. It was 2 o'clock in the morning, one of our neighbours wake us up with a hard knock. He was coming home from his night–shift and found all the door mats from other 4 flats been put together in front of our door and set fire.

He ran to get water from his flat to wake us up. Oh! It was a horrible feeling. We could see fire already inside our hallway. Both of us felt so helpless and hold sleeping Lali tightly. Why it had to happen to us? Next door neighbours were very helpful. I started to think how we are bring up Lali in this racist environment? Next night we heard a big bang on our door, then straighway we left the flat in our sleeping dress and stayed with our friend. We were very friendly with the neighbours—never faced any sort of harassment. Definitely someone hated us so badly—who did not even hesitate to burn us while we were sleeping with Lali. We were the only Asian family there.

Police were not very helpful. They found it quite difficult to identify what sort of incident it was. But my husband did not let them get away like this. He contacted the Police Chief of the borough and made it clear himself to the police what sort of incident it was. It was out of question to go back and lived in the same place again—council was not helpful about rehousing.

Still today, we think who don't speak English and mix well—what sort of treatment they get from this racist society and police. We people just want to work hard, earn money and look after family here, as well as back home.

After few months staying with our friends, we bought our house and moved. One thing I realise it is our friends from back home really help us when we are in desperate situation, rather than anyone else. I mean plenty of lip sympathy, not a real help.

So long I will live, always try my best to forget that horrifying experience of two nights. It is unfortunate because of the economic condition of our country and family responsibility back home. I am trying to settle here and want to live in harmony with majority community. Now I am a British citizen.

Last summer while my husband went to West Germany for a conference, we accompanied him. There the German border–guard picked up a point that my passport does not carry a stamp that the holder has a right of abode in U.K. He refused a British passport holder by putting a refused seal. The only reason one can put for this, is the colour of my skin, Black. As my husband made a protest through our local M.P. made a headline in local and National newspaper, it came to a light. We did receive a letter of apology from German Immigration Authority—still that racist attitude of the white race so obvious.

A spokesman for the home office confirmed that the Nationality Act which came into force in January '84 altered the wording in the front of all British passports issued after 31st December '83.

With all these sorts of incidents one has to think always whether it will be at all possible for me to feel at home in this country and feel this to be as my home. People don't know how many black people are suffering. So many ways—it is just not anybody's business.

FARIDA

Demonstrating against their friend's threatened deportation

[illegible]

[illegible] আমি আমার স্বামীর সাথে লন্ডনে আসি। আমাদের [illegible] আছে।

[illegible] আমি [illegible] ছিলাম। [illegible]

[illegible] আমার [illegible] ও [illegible]

[illegible] আমার [illegible] ও [illegible] আমার [illegible]

[illegible]

আমার [illegible] আমি আমার স্বামীর [illegible] আমার [illegible]

আমার স্বামী "[illegible]" [illegible] ডি, এইচ, এস [illegible] ডি, এইচ, এস [illegible] আমার [illegible]

Like every other woman, some things I do, I do everyday—getting the children to school, breakfast, shopping, going to work, cooking. In between I do have my social and cultural life. You will see some in my pictures. It is not that always it is boring, my job brings me into contact with different people. It makes interesting. Definitely I wouldn't like without a job. I'm not a person to be happy only if I stay indoors, that's why I get myself involved with my daughter's school and within my own community.

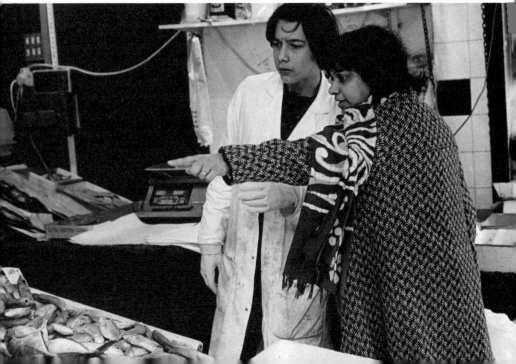

THE MINIMUM OF CONTACT

The new life which I was to encounter in Britain for the next fifteen years began with my arrival to London in July 1968. I came at the age of nine with my mother and brother to join my father who came to London a year earlier.

The four of us set up our first home in the vicinity of Euston. Our home consisted of one large and dilapidated room. We shared the kitchen and bathroom facilities with other people. The location and condition of our lodging prompted us to move out. Within one month we found another more comfortable lodging. It was located in Islington, London N.1.

At about this time, my brother and I joined a local primary school. In the beginning, both of us found the school environment strange because of our inability to communicate with most of the people around us. However, we found some people who were sympathetic towards us and helped us to settle in. One such person was our English teacher. Whenever we attended his classes, we received extra help in learning the language. Our ability to speak English improved further by the activities we undertook outside of school. Our father always encouraged and sometimes forced us to go shopping alone and to mix with the other children in the street.

After spending two years together in the same school, my brother and I were separated. I left to join a secondary school whilst my brother remained in the junior school for a further year. The transition from primary to secondary school ran less smoothly for me than it did for most of my friends. When the time came for choosing secondary schools, the parents of all pupils were requested to fill in application forms stating the names of three schools of their choice in their order of preference. My father chose three local girls' school, but none of them accepted me. Instead I was placed in a mixed school. An explanation was offered for the action by the headmaster, who told my father that vacancies for places at the schools of my choice were all filled. However, my father was dissatisfied and threatened to keep me at home until a suitable girls' school was found for me. The matter was settled shortly when ILEA intervened with the suggestion that I join the school of my third choice. Looking back now, I cannot decide whether to consider this particular incident as discriminatory or not.

At the school, I had to adjust to a new way of life for I no longer had the company or support of my brother. Being shy and reserved in nature from a very early age, I found difficulty in making friends. Slowly, I overcame this inhibition and mixed with several girls. There were two with whom I grew particularly close. Both were English and their names were Lynne and Susan. Although I became fond of the two girls, I did not approve of their family life. Both of them had parents who gave little attention to their academic progress. This mode of behaviour was in sharp contrast to that of my own parents who cared a great deal about my school work. Consequently, I felt ashamed to discuss too enthusiastically about my friends with my parents lest they should disapprove and at no time did I ever bring either of them home with me to introduce to my parents.

Outside of school, I mixed with the children in my street most of whom belonged to immigrant families like myself. I always felt more comfortable in the company of Asian or African children.

At about this time my family moved house again. After 10 months we went to live in a two—bedroomed flat in the same area. We remained there for a further two and a half years before moving into a newly purchased house nearby.

At the age of fifteen, I suddenly began to experience certain emotional upheavals that are normally associated with people of this age. My feelings were divided: on the one hand I was tempted to follow the casual lifestyles of my friends and at the same time I was compelled to stay loyal to the respectable Indian way of life of my parents. I confided this problem to my closest friend, Susan. She could not help me directly but introduced me to two other girls both of whom were pupils at my school. The four of us discussed the matter at length, and reached the conclusion that I should leave home. For several weeks after the idea initially entered my head, I felt restless. Then gradually, I grew accustomed to it and made the necessary plans. Finally, one day, I approached the three girls to ask for their help. At this stage, Susan who had originally planned to leave home with me changed her mind and decided to stay behind. She also tried in vain to deter me from going. One of the girls suggested that I go to Brighton to stay with her aunt. There I would be able to obtain a job and never be found by my parents. The final arrangement seemed so appealing that one day without informing my parents and taking only several necessary items, I packed a bag and left. I spent that first day and night staying at the flat of one of the girls. The following morning the three of us went to Victoria Station where we boarded a train to Brighton. When we reached our destination, however, we were disappointed not to find the aunt at home. So we decided to return home for the time being and try our luck the following day. That evening I experienced the most harrowing time of my life. Neither of the two girls wanted to shelter me for the night in their homes for fear of their mothers becoming suspicious of my presence.

Left to face an evening without shelter, I walked around the streets of various places in London. When night came, I felt tired and so decided to settle down somewhere until the morning. The safest place for hiding at that time was the basement floor of the block of flats where one of the girls lived. The place was hidden from public view and allowed easy access to my friend's flat in case of an emergency. Once settled in, I felt cold, uncomfortable and unable to fall asleep. I stayed awake for the greater part of the night feeling drowsy. I also experienced a feeling of despair and for the first time since the incident began, I was frightened at the thought of never seeing my parents again. I wondered whether it was right to run away from them just because they failed to understand me. Between conflicting thoughts, I managed to catch snatches of sleep. That miserable night seemed never ending and when it finally melted away, I faced the morning with renewed hope. At first break of daylight, I went upstairs to call on my friend who promptly invited me in. Meanwhile, her mother slipped out of the flat with the excuse that she had to buy a newspaper. Some time after her return, came the police. I was then taken by car to a nearby police station and kept there until the arrival of my parents.

When I returned home that day accompanied by my parents I felt safe once more and grateful for the way the whole incident ended. Most of all, I felt ashamed for having caused a lot of misery to two of the most kindest and caring people I have ever known.

As soon as I recovered from that ordeal, I joined a new school. My father, with the help of my tutor at the old school, arranged for me to be transferred to another school.

Ironically, this was the school I most wanted to go to straight from my primary school. Indeed I had placed its name at the top of the list of secondary schools of my choice when asked to fill in the appropriate application forms. It was then considered to be the most disciplined of all girls' comprehensive schools in the borough of Islington.

This school possessed a kind of orderliness which the other school lacked, but the academic achievements of the pupils there were lower than in my old school. The change in school at this crucial period of my life had an adverse effect on my studies. Some of the subjects which I had studied at my own school for the first year of a two-year 'O' level course were no longer available to me at this school. Consequently, I was forced to take up new subjects to replace them half way through the course. Added to the enormous changes in study patterns were the adjustments I had to make to new friendships with teachers and pupils.

At this school, I was careful not to make too many friends and certainly not to fall under any of their bad influences. Fortunately, two of the four girls with whom I managed to pick up friendship with were foreigners like myself. One of them was a Greek−Cypriot girl called Christella and the other called Leona came from St. Lucia. The two remaining friends; Janice and Jackie were both English. Janice was a quiet girl from a good family.

I developed a meaningful relationship with Leona. We shared something in common; both of us had a serious outlook. In fact, I got on so amicably with her that she was the only person from my school-days with whom I still maintain contact.

1977 was the year I left school. It was also the year of another important change, for in September my father went abroad. He entered into a contract with the government of Nigeria to work as teacher for three years in their country. The news of his intended departure came as a shock to the rest of the family especially to my mother who was soon to be left with the burden of supporting two children.

The summer months of 1978, 1979 and 1980 were the most memorable occasions in my life. In July 1978 I went outside of Britain for the first time in ten years. In India, I met some of my relatives and witnessed the poverty stricken life styles of most of the ordinary citizens. During the summers of 1979 and 1980, our journeys to India included short stop−overs in a number of countries. These were the USA, Japan, Switzerland, West Germany, Italy, Holland, Thailand, Burma, Indonesia, Hong Kong, Singapore and Ceylon. Looking back now, it seems that those few months of tour helped me to understand a little about the world and the contrasting life styles of some of the people who inhabit it. Nigeria in particular left an unforgettable impression in my mind and heart. For it was a country with breathtaking natural beauty. Its vast, barren and unspoilt land reminded me of how beautiful the world was before Man began to destroy it in the name of progress.

After spending one year at College, I left disappointed with the quality of teaching. With the hope of receiving better tuition, I joined an independent college. The fees at the college came to approximately £1,000, all of which was paid for by my parents. At the end of a year at Holborn, I sat the 'A' level examinations. I failed to pass in any of the three subjects, but the results did not prevent me from trying again. Disappointed with my experiences at this college, I left to join another further educational college in South London. In all of the three institutions, I found the quality of tuition and the attitude of teachers in general very unsatisfactory. At the end of the following year, I resat the 'A' levels, this time obtaining better grades. However, the grades were too low for the purposes of university entrance. Since my departure from college in 1980, I have continued my studies at home with the help of private tutors. Just recently, I sat the 'A' levels for another time with the hope of success. If it comes then I will join a suitable university to study for the BSc degree in Biochemistry.

MITA

(A year later this is how Mita felt)

In retrospect, the days of my childhood were a mixture of good and bad times. I experienced the good times during my early life until the mid−teens. At that time, I carried little of the worries that burden my life today. I enjoyed the companionships offered by my school friends and almost totally under their influence. I craved for their friendship and attention and gave very little thought to the feelings of my parents. At times when my parents reprimanded me severely, I would feel anger and hate towards them, (especially towards my father who was always more strict than my mother). I conveyed those unhappy feelings to my friends whom I trusted more than my parents and was eventually persuaded by them to run away from home.

As I grew older my attitude towards my friends and parents gradually changed. I found that my parents' behaviour towards me mellowed with time. The events which caused me to leave home had taught both parties, myself and my parents, how much misunderstanding existed among us. As their attitudes changed, I felt more comfortable with them. I began to realise that their concern for me was more genuine than that of my friends.

By the time I had reached the sixth form I became almost disinterested in friendships and was more concerned about passing exams and building a secure future for myself. When I left school to join a further education college, I was careful not to become too involved with people. That transitory phase was the most difficult I have encountered in life so far. It was the first time when I was totally alone to face a world which proved to be very hostile. In the beginning I missed the carefree and sheltered life of school. The teachers at the new institution were less caring than those at school. Their unconcerned attitudes and my reluctance to make friends in the new environment left me with feelings of loneliness and insecurity. Further unhappiness was added to my life that year when my father left for Nigeria. Although I was more free in his absence, I always remained worried for his well−being. During that time, I grew more fond of my mother especially when I saw how much effort she made to provide the support needed by my brother and myself to establish our careers. I was able to talk freely with her about my ambitions and her to be more sympathetic and understanding than my father.

The results from my first ever public examinations proved disappointing. Of the eight subjects for which I took the CSE, I passed with the top most grade in just two. The bad results made me realise that despite my youthful age, I had very little time left in which to build a career. I had seen the plight of the majority of girls who left school without acquiring any worthwhile academic qualifications. They entered professions like secretarial, shop, hospital and factory work. I had no taste for such jobs. My intention was to build a career which will not only bring security in future but also enable me to eventually leave this country. By that time, I had experienced enough of life to realise that I could not fit into this society. From then onwards I began slowly to withdraw contact from all aspects of this society. Even to this day, I try to maintain the minimum of contact.

I left school in 1977 after acquiring five 'O' levels. That meagre qualification was considered enough to get myself into the further education college. I enrolled to study for the 'A' level course in Physics, Chemistry and Biology. My father tried his utmost to make me alter my choice. He would have been happier to see me study for some 'A' level arts subjects simply because in his estimation I was incapable of handling such academically difficult subjects.

Until the time I entered Tottenham College, my father was very strict in his dealings with my brother and myself. He always tried to run our lives the way he thought fit. He gave little regard to our feelings or wishes. Sometimes he would even beat us if we disobeyed him or expressed displeasure towards any of his suggestions. Consequently, both of us kept out of his way as far as possible. In contrast, my mother was kind, considerate and gentle. She was more approachable and therefore we were better able to communicate our thoughts with her.

Whilst my father was in Nigeria, I felt a little insecure but free. He often wrote to me explaining about the hardships he was having to endure on foreign land as well as the rewards he was receiving for his labour. One of those rewards was a holiday at the end of each working year. During such holidays my mother, brother and I flew to Nigeria to meet him. Then, the four of us together flew back to Britain where we rested for several days before flying to India. The air fare for those extensive trips were paid by the Nigerian Government.

In the six years since leaving school, I have managed to acquire some 'O' and 'A' levels which have enabled me to enter higher education. I am now studying for the BSc in Chemistry and hope to graduate in a few years time. Nowadays, the parental influence in my life is very little. My parents know me to be a very private person and therefore leave me alone most of the time. As for the future, I hope to return to India soon after gaining sufficient academic qualifications. Having visited India on several occasions since my first arrival to this country I feel more akinned to the society over there than to the society in this country.

Now my parents are thinking of my marriage.

Yes, they asked whether I want to and what sort of man I like as well. After going through all the ups and downs I want to settle in India. But at the same time, when thinking about the material side, if my dream does not come out true I shall have to come back with my husband. So I need a British Passport before I go to India for marriage. Though after years of painful experience I strongly feel "It is not worth giving up my Indian nationality to this country"—been born in a poor country there is no choice left.

Maya and Jalpa

OUR ONLY IDENTITY

My husband went to India to get married after staying here three years. I was in my post–graduate class—it was completely arranged marriage. I will be honest I was thrilled—having no man friend before I did not have any problem to adjust with him—as I came to London I did not have to put up with any everyday's formalities in my in–law's house.

As he was before, after staying few days with his brother, we moved to a nice council flat—I gave birth to our son Babul. It was a three storey house. Ground floor was let to an old lady around 60 years.

By the way, now day by day, all the dreams, of newly married girl come to make home in "the land of peace and money", started to fade. Cold weather and pressure of life I felt very low.

Though I was not fluent in my English and been home whole day with my son I tried to make friendship with my neighbour, as she was on her own, also as same age as my aunt (who spent all her life in our family when she became widow at age 13 years). I felt concern about her well being. We used the same corridor. If I had not seen her I knocked her door and asked about her health and whether she needs any shopping. I was shocked when she thought I am being nosey and became rude. I started to go out more meet few neighbours on the street and came to know how horrible inconsiderate noisy people we are. My son started walk now. Though we furnish our living room we never asked any friends in our flat. Always we used to go to my brother–in–law's house during weekends. She felt degraded as she was housed with us. My husband and me are keen gardeners—we shared the garden and there was a fence. Our side was really beautiful. Whenever she saw us started to shout "go back home, Blacki etc". Now for my son we just somehow finish our use of kitchen and went to end floor. Does not matter and we could not even sneeze—always complaining noise—I started to lose weight and so many times I beat my son, though hardly he was allowed to come to kitchen—We moved our T.V. in the bedroom. My husband become very quiet person, tried to move out but council not helpful.

Because of the price we could not afford buying our own place. We just could not stand it anymore—Luckily I found a place for my son in the nursery though it was not our actual plan to put him there at age of 2 years. I found a job in a dress factory. Every penny was saved within one year we moved to our new house. Now we talk, laugh, watch T.V. and our son can play in garden—Yes, he can have his meal in our big kitchen. We feel so guilty about him because of pressure I beat him so many times. But three years haunting experience made me wake up at the middle of night still that knock on our floor.

My new neighbours are okay so far—I am sometimes so frightened about English people and feel they don't see anything good in us. Just we are black bastards, that is our only identity.

MANDIRA

મંદિરા   *Mandira* 'આપણી ખરી ઓળખ'

મારા પતિ આ દેશમાં ઝાઝા વર્ષ રહ્યા પછી ભારત લગ્ન કરવા માટે આવ્યા હતા. તે વખતે હું પોસ્ટ ગ્રેજ્યુએટનો અભ્યાસ કરતી હતી. અમારા લગ્ન વડીલોની સંમતિથી ગોઠવાયેલ (Arranged) લગ્ન હતા. મારા લગ્નનો મને પૂરજ આનંદ હતો. લગ્ન પહેલા મારે બીજા કોઈ પુરુષ સાથે ભિન્નગારી ન હોવાથી મારા પતિ સાથે ગોઠવાઈ જતા મને જરાય મુશ્કેલી ન પડી. અને લગ્ન પછી તરત જ અહિં આવી જવાથી ભારતના મારા આસપડિયાના ટોળાંના વ્યવહારથી પણ અને છૂટકારો મળી ગયો.

લગ્ન પછી આ દેશમાં આવીને અમે થોડો વખત મારા પતિના ભાઈને ઘેર રહ્યા. ત્યારપછી અમે અમારા પોતાના કાઉન્સિલના ફ્લેટમાં રહેવા લાગ્યા. ઝાઝા માળના મોટા મકાનમાં અમારો ફ્લેટ હતો. નીચેના માળે લગભગ ૬૦ વર્ષની ઉંમરની એક વૃદ્ધ અંગ્રેજ સ્ત્રી રહેતી હતી. કાઉન્સિલના આ ફ્લેટમાં રહેવા આવ્યા પછી મારા દિકરા 'બાબુલ'નો જન્મ થયો.

પ્રત્યેક ભારતીય નવોઢાને પોતાનો સુખી સંસાર વસાવવાના સ્વપ્ન હોય છે તેમ મને પણ આ પરાયા સમૃદ્ધ દેશ ઈંગ્લેંડમાં મારો સુખી સંસાર વસાવવાના સ્વપ્ન હતા. પરંતુ આ સ્વપ્નો ધીરે ધીરે નષ્ટ થતા લાગ્યા. આ દેશના ધુમ્મસિયા ગગનથી અને અભિશાપ કંકા હવામાનથી મારા મનનાં ઉમળકો અળશી થવા લાગ્યા.

મને અંગ્રેજી ભાષા બરાબર આવડતી ન હતી. આખો દિવસ મારા દીકરા સાથે હું ઘર એકલી રહેતી હતી. જીવન ખૂબ એકલવાયું લાગતું હોવાથી મેં મારા પડોશી વૃદ્ધા અંગ્રેજ બાઈ સાથે મિત્રાચારી બાંધી. આ બાઈ મને મારા પોતાના દીકરીની યાદ અપાવતા હતા. મારા દીકરી આ બાઈની ઉંમરના લગભગ હતા પરંતુ તેર વર્ષની નાની ઉંમરે જ વિધવા થતા બાકીનું આખું જીવન તેમણે અમારા કુટુંબમાં રહીને જ ગુજાર્યું હતું.

મારા પડોશી વૃદ્ધા બાઈની સલામતીનો હું ખ્યાલ રાખતી હતી. જો થોડો સમય એમના દર્શન ન થાય તો એમને દરવાજે ખખડાવીને હું એમની ખબરઅંતર પૂછતી હતી. બહારથી કોઈ વસ્તુ ખરીદવાની હોય તો એ વિષે પણ હું પૂછતી. પણ ધીરે ધીરે મને ખબર પડવા લાગી કે મારું આવું મિત્રાચારી ભર્યું વર્તન આ બાઈને જરાપણ પસંદ ન હતું. એના રોજિંદા જીવન-વ્યવહારમાં વારંવાર એની ખબરઅંતર પૂછીને હું દખલ કરું એ એને જરાય ગમતું નહિ. આ વાતની જાણ થતા મને પણ દુઃખી થઈ નવાઈ લાગી.

ધીરે ધીરે હું બહારના લોકો સાથે ભળવા લાગી. મારા પડોશી બાઈ અમને ખૂબ દમામિયા, અવાજ કરનાર અને એમનો જરાય વિચાર ન કરનાર માનવા લાગ્યા. આ સમયગાળા

દરમ્યાન મારો દીકરો ચાલતા પણ શીખ્યો અને અમારું દિવાનખાનું ફર્નીશ કર્યું હતું પરંતુ અમારા પડોશીની હરકતને લઈને અમે અમારા કોઈ મિત્રમંડળને અમારે ઘેર આમંત્રણ આપી શકતા નહિ. દરેક અઠવાડિયાને અંતે (વીક એન્ડ) અમે મારા પતિના આવીને ઘેર જ ચાલી જતા.

જે મકાનમાં અમે રહીએ એ એક મકાનમાં એ બાઈને રહેવું પડતું હતું તે એને જરાય પસંદ ન હતું. અમારા ગાર્ડનના વચ્ચે વાડ કરીને બે ભાગ કરવામાં આવ્યા હતા. એક ભાગનું એમના હક્કનું અને એક ભાગ અમારો હતો. હું અને મારા પતિ ગાર્ડનમાં ઘણો રસ ધરાવતા હતા અને ઘણો સમય ફાળવીને એમાં કામ કરતા તેથી અમારું ગાર્ડન ઘણું સુંદર રહેતું.

આ વૃદ્ધ બાઈ જ્યારે પણ અમને જોતી ત્યારે બોલવા લાગતી કે 'ફોરેનર્સ! તમે તમારા દેશમાં ચાલી જાઓ.' રસોડાનું કામ વહેલાસર વહેલું પતાવીને મારા બાબાને લઈને હું બીજે માળે ચાલી જતી. અમે ટીંખવા જેટલો અવાજ પણ કરી શકતા નહિ. જ્યારે જુઓ ત્યારે આ બાઈ, 'અમે ખૂબ દમામ અને અવાજ કરીએ છીએ' એવીજ ફરિયાદ કરતી હતી. એના અમારા પ્રત્યેના આવા વર્તનથી મારા જીવનમાં ઘણી માઠી અસર પડી. મારા વજનમાં ઘટાડો થવા લાગ્યો. હું અવારનવાર વગર કારણે મારા બાબાને મારવા લાગી. એ જરાય અવાજ ન કરે માટે એને રસોડામાં પણ આવવા ન દેતી. અમે અમારું ટી.વી. દિવાનખાનાને બદલે

સૂવાના ઓરડામાં રાખવા માંડ્યુ. મારા પતિનો સ્વભાવ પણ ખૂબ શાંત થઈ ગયો. અને કાઉન્સિલમાં બીજે બદલી માટે માગણી કરી તો એનો પણ ઈનકાર કરવામાં આવ્યો.

મકાનોની મોટી કિંમત અને અમારી આર્થિક પરિસ્થિતિ બહુ સારી ન હોવાથી પોતાનું મકાન ખરીદવાની કોઈ શક્યતા ન હતી. અમારી પડોશણા બાઈનું વર્તન અમારા પ્રત્યે એટલું કનડગતભર્યું હતું કે અમે વધારે સહન કરી શકીએ એમ હતું જ નહિ.

નસીબયોગે મારા દિકરાને નર્સરીમાં જગા મળી. નાની બે વર્ષની ઉંમરે એ બાળકને નર્સરીમાં મૂકવાની ઈચ્છા ન હોવા છતાં પરિસ્થિતિ અને સંજોગોથી મજબૂર થઈને અમે એને નર્સરીમાં દાખલ કર્યો. મેં પોતે ફ્રેંચ ટ્યુટરમાં કામ કરવાની કરૂણાત કરી. શક્ય એટલી બધી બચત કરીને એક વર્ષના ગાળામાં અમે પોતાનું મકાન ખરીદ્યું. હવે હસવા, બોલવાની, ટી.વી. જોવાની બીધી મજા અને ફોઈપણા અડચણ વિના માણી શકીએ છીએ. અમારો દિકરો ગાર્ડનમાં છૂટથી દરીદુરી અને રમી શકે છે. રસોડામાં તેમીને શાંતિથી જમી શકે છે.

છેલ્લા ત્રણ વર્ષના ગાળામાં મેં એને ઘણી વાર વિના કારણે માર્યો છે એનો મને ખરેખર ખૂબ જ અફસોસ થાય છે. ગત ત્રણ વર્ષોનો કડવો અનુભવ આજે પણ મને ઘણીવાર ઊંઘમાંથી સફાળી જગાડી મૂકે છે.

અમારા નવા અંગ્રેજ પડોશી હજુ સુધી તો ઘણા સારા છે છતાં અંગ્રેજ લોકોનો મને ઘણીવાર ખૂબ જ ડર લાગે છે. તેઓ આપણામાં કોઈ 'સારાપણું' જોઈ શકતા નથી. આપણી ચામડીયો તેઓની નજરમાં કાળા, નાલાયક અને અણગમતા જ છીએ. આજ આપણી ખરી 'ઓળખ' અંગ્રેજ લોકોને છે.

WHEN LIFE GOT ROUGH

I am an Asian girl of 19 years and I am a student. I have siblings but do not wish to reveal our identity.

My parents got divorced 2 years ago because my father is an alcoholic and wife batterer. The decree absolute came through two months before my parents 25th wedding anniversary.

As a consequence of my parents' divorce, we the children, have been the target of discussion and gossip in our community. My mother faces hardship too with rumours within the community, but since the divorce life has been more peaceful.

My mother married at 14 years because her parents thought it fit. They had found a young man from a wealthy family who could feed and clothe her. As long as a woman had these things in life along with somewhere to live, she needed nothing else—love played a small part in marriage. My father being fairly well off followed the pattern of most men in his neighbourhood and started drinking heavily. On the good days he'd stagger home at about 2.00 pm in the afternoon, drunk out of his mind and go straight to bed. On a bad day he'd batter my mother. When they came to England my mother thought he'd stop, instead he drank more and when life got rough, so did he. Life wasn't easy for Asians in the '60s, but both my parents worked and brought us children over to join them, then they bought a house.

All the while the drinking and battering went on, until my mother began to see sense. She realised that she could no longer live with an alcoholic, we, the children were often frightened of him and wished him dead. Many is the time she left him with the children and stayed with relatives. She even started divorce proceedings but he tracked us down and brought us back home. Vowing that he'd never drink or beat my mother again. However, these promises soon slipped his mind and we were back to square one. This did very little for us because our standard of work was low and we were too engrossed in domestic problems to concentrate on our school work. In 1978 my mother made the final decision and left my father again, this time for good. We lived at two addresses for 2 years until we were sure that the divorce would be granted.

Since the divorce we have achieved a great deal. The scholars in the family are doing well, the house has been re−decorated and modernised where necessary and our lives are so much more comfortable. When my father was home we had very few suitors for marriage but now we have a lot more, although my mother insists that there is a lot more to life than marriage. My mother was not sure about getting a divorce because she knew that if she did, the children would be left penniless. But that's not a problem because we'd sooner have nothing without him, than everything with him.

I believe that if I worked for something and earned it, then I can call it mine. If I inherit something, it's what my relatives worked for. It's best for each person to make their own path in life, so why need what belongs to your parents?

As usual people find fault in the way we are being brought up. "It wouldn't be like that if their father was still there", is the usual comment that gets back to us. People feel that we are being treated too 'mildly' we have 'too much freedom'. Well I think we have just enough to keep us within our culture.

If you bring a child up too strictly, that child will run free at the first chance it gets. This means that if a child is dictated to, has no privacy and is condemned to the house, she will either rebel or marry the first Tom, Dick, or Harry who comes along. If he's her type of guy that's fine, if not, hard luck!

I know people who listen sympathetically are the ones who sneer and criticise us behind our backs. We have met quite a bit of hostility because of the divorce. Some people find my mother a cruel and ruthless woman to have divorced my father, and he's such a sweet, sociable man, when he's sober.

My mother isn't the only woman who had such a husband, there are others out there. They get battered week, after week, for trivial reasons. Some husbands are alcoholics, but others do it sober. It happens with young and middle aged couples, but the women are too scared to divorce. They are frightened of the outside world, the courts and lawyers, the documents they probably won't understand, and most of all they fear their family.

The families will feud and look down on her. She'll lose her friends. She'll have nowhere to go. If she's illiterate she'll find more problems. So to avoid all this hassle, she will stay with her husband. That way she nor her parents will face any shame.

Courage is really what it boils down to, whether or not a woman has the courage to live as she wants to, instead of under the order of a battering husband. Can she decide what's best for her when she's torn between duty and freedom. Even if she can, she won't do much about it, she lacks guts and common sense!

To many Europeans marriage is a way of life, so is divorce. If two people cannot live together in peace, then why do so?

Although divorce is quite easy to come by it does not and shouldn't make a marriage vulnerable to break—up. I believe, as many, that marriage is a sacred institution and a couple should hold on together as long as possible. I don't want to marry more than once, I want one husband and a family to raise in a cosy home. I would like my husband to be of my religion at least and know him for a few years before settling down.

Many people still believe that his or her partner can be located in the stars through an astrologer, who will give descriptions or initials of the mysterious partner. This is so romantic and exciting, but what if the stars chosen are not your lucky stars?

My personal view is that you are not on this earth to fulfil the wishes of others. You have a life and feelings of your own. You have rights as a human being, rights that shouldn't be taken away by any other person. No one knows what hardships you face and you can never please everybody so "please yourself".

I look around me and can see jealousy filling in people. How dare we get on so well without my father, and achieve so much. They are jealous because we can progress better than them. We are a happy family which is more than what I can say for some.

People judge us, pass comments on how we've turned out, what we do and how we do things. Who are these people to judge, they are not my maker. What right do they have to judge me, why, what wrong have I done to them? How does my way of living affect them?

As Christ once put it "Let he who has never sinned, cast the first stone."

In this case no one has sinned, the person who judges me to their standard, sins first.

DIPU

YOU CANNOT DO IT ALONE

I am Indian brought up in India but I am living in London since I was 12 years of age. I was brought up here by my father who is Indian and a European step—mother and two step—brothers. I had such understanding parents and of course westernised ways in thinking as well as in outlook that I had very few problems adjusting to English society in general. Although I knew no English when I arrived in this country I soon learnt and mastered the language within a year, only with a lot of help from my step—mother and from school.

I am a qualified S.R.N. and at present divorced with two very young children. I made this difficult decision after 5 years of marriage and after a great deal of thought and consideration. I married a man of my choice but despite that when things got too unbearable I had no alternative but to make this decision and take care of my children alone, for their sake as well as for my own.

I am writing about this experience as any divorced woman would. It is not easy but mentally bearable and once the situation is accepted from within oneself and to ignore the stigma which is attached to the single parent family, you are halfway to success and feel on top of .the world again, but remember that you cannot do it alone. I was lucky, very, very lucky indeed to have such understanding parents who helped me a great deal, listened to my problems, gave me their time, tremendous strength and precious moments. It was such help and acceptance that I began to see the light ahead of me. I am now quite settled in my house and in my feelings. My children are happy with their grandparents, I am happy with friends and with life in general. The children see their father once a week but there are no tears now. The burning fire has died out and only the ashes have been left behind.

It is up to me now to make something of my life. As I said without good friends and my parents I would not have gone through this 'experience without a breakdown. I would advise any woman especially an Asian where the parents would not accept such a decision to get as much help as possible from the Marriage Guidance counsellor. Remember girls that you are not alone and you need not suffer if you have the courage and strength and tremendous will power, that is the key to success.

TO BE LITTLE BRAVE AND FLEXIBLE

Prejudice is something; everybody suffer with it in different shapes. Some people very strong about their own food. They won't eat anything but their own. Some people don't want their children to mix or play with the neighbour's children because they play on the footpath. Without realising they live in a small flat.

This avoiding and not mixing only create between the two parties a big wall. It is understandable that different culture have got different ways of thinking and different way of life. That don't mean we can't be friends. You just have to be little brave and flexible to accept someone's else who is not look alike you, who don't eat the same food as you neither speak your language. So straight away quite a few barriers to overcome, not easy. Perhaps lot of people without much efforts try to get on with their own life with prejudice or fear inside them. It is worse and sad in lot of cases it turn into hatred.

More than 16 years ago when I came here and today, now look back. My feeling is lot of people around me during that time were helpful, some were curious and anxious and very few people tried to be funny and bit rude. When I started to work as a clerical assistant at Ministry of Transport my first friend was Frank, he was in his sixties. His wife worked in the same building as well. But it took Mollie few years to accept us. They live at Twickenham. Frank asked us for a lunch. Mollie came to me few times at my office to know what we eat or not again phoned me at home at least three times to know the same things. I felt Mollie's anxious and wanted to avoid the lunch but because of Frank could not avoid it. Now Mollie is a great friend too. But it was quite effort for her at first to accept us. Frank had to come our part of London for his brother—always popped in, Mollie sat in the car and parked it far. Though long time now Frank never try Indian food and Mollie loved it, I could not make Frank take even a pinch of curry—so it is nothing but sort of fear. But I will remember his help and affection in that cold and artificial environment at my first office.

Also, after 9 years when I was moved to Mr. Martin I come to realise the word "racist". He never call like everybody else, always Mrs. Manju. Often came to stand behind me, watching me—oh it was horrible feeling. The job I was doing was known to me luckily—so he did not get chance to catch me on that ground though he tried his best. One West Indian boy tried to hit him before he went back to university. I won't blame Garry. After 2/3 months I had to go to our Higher Executive Officer and ask for transfer. No coloured people could work under him but so far I know he never been called by personnel or warned for his attitude. It was so cold, direct prejudice I suffer few months of my life I won't forget.

MANJU

অ। কিন্তু প্রবন্ধ দি কে উঠ গুরুত্বপূর্ণ হল
ক্ষেত্রাংশে ভার কেন উঠ বিষ তব স্বীকার ।
দি ছোটবে কবিন নেতৃত্ব ও সংকীর্ণতা
ভাবনা নতুন ক্ষেত্রপন নেতৃত্ব — সকল সংগ্রাম
এ রেখে পথ ।

FIGHT BACK WITH WORDS

What does 'being an Indian' mean to me? A complex question with perhaps no simple answers. The nearest I can get to it is by saying, it is a way of life for me. A cultural experience not outside the influence of an Anglicised culture. I have been married to an English person since 5 years and have lived in England all this time (with a long visit with Brian to India for a period of 5 months). He has lived in India before (that is when I met him) and speaks Tamil. This is to illustrate some familiarity on his part with the Indian way of life—albeit—of some significance to his actual understanding of another culture other than his own. We share common views and experiences of our political understanding and life.

As I see my experiences having very close links to my life as an Indian woman and the close harmony of two cultures in shaping my political thought, I must admit to having limited my horizons somewhat. I feel quite close to many things I have learnt and assimilated in my life since I left the home of my parents. These ideas had begun to emerge as I protested vociferously in my own name and idealistic youthful way against arranged marriage, dowry, poverty and social inequalities, the rich, the poor, the servants in the homes of the rich, Indian bureaucracy and the role of the state as I saw it then. I gained very little support but always being placed in a position of being on trial for holding such views, I learnt to fight back with words. So I learnt to speak and responded by formulating quite strong views on the Indian way of life. I went on to study architecture which taught me two things—(1) To realise I was getting deeper into the very system that I was fighting, since it is a profession not common to women and is practised on behalf of the wealthy and powerful men; I was learning the nature of the opposition of ideas, as my work brought me in touch with powerful people. Matters were made complicated by the fact that my 'enemies' were people close to me. (Having 'shameful' wealthy connections myself I could not avoid this situation.) (2) I had wasted my time at school but had learnt various bits and pieces about myself and politics. These ideas and a desire to live by some of them at least made me choose to leave behind what I then saw as traditional strangleholds which were constraining me from 'growing'. Moreover, I had made a promise to myself that I would never subject myself to the indignity of being 'given away' like some property. (In truth I grew up as the daughter of the house 'who was someone' else's 'property' to be given away during Kanyadaan—the sacrifice of the daughter.) So my parents were being gently, and often not so gently (blazing arguments with my father in particular and emotional scenes) persuaded to see my point of view and had begun to accept some of it.

A long complex process filled with doubt, enthusiasm growth of awareness of many things has been accompanying me—which is very difficult to relate in this context. However, I saw it fit to project some kind of sketch to enable appreciation of the present context.

Recently I have come into contact with the ideas emerging in the Indian Women's movement which coincides with my work (unfortunately mostly of an academic nature) on the role of Indian women during the Indian struggle against British Imperialism and I must say Imperialism as an ideology is an entity I have always found myself in conflict with. I connect this with my everyday awareness of life in Brightlingsea (a beautiful old seaside town with a very friendly community of people and small enterprises. In the old part where I live everybody knows of everybody else's existence). I feel very much at home since I am accepted at a 'superficial' level. I am the Indian women by an image which I project in isolation of any Indian community. This is quite problematic in coming to terms with. I am Indian, therefore by something more than a physical image of me, so no matter how I dressed I still represent something 'Indian' and it is this that I try to define for myself. The work on the history of imperialism in India and the struggles of Indian women bear close links with the ideas which influenced my awareness. This brings me in conflict with Brian—amongst other levels of conflict—as we evolve our live through the contradictions we live with: each other and the 'others' out of the conflict emerges more understanding about me, this way I resolve my differences with people at various levels.

Perhaps I am not saying anything new but what I say is relevant to the way I perceive my life. In the Indian community who knows me I am viewed on the basis of assumptions about the English people and vice versa. This is quite complex to work with in view of my own needs to reject most of what both these cultures represent since cultures are not created in isolation of people who have dominated them through history. So what? Well, I don't see these experiences in isolation from the experiences of women involved in some struggle somewhere with similar aspirations whatever differences we may have in following different routes. I seek to combine experiences and also seek to define the nature of the struggle. The fact that I find myself in conflict implies there are some things I must reject and others I must accept.

I try to recreate the 'extended family' feeling that is so much a part of a Gujerati patidan's life by emphasizing certain needs of my friends and have an 'open house' atmosphere which I value so much about the Indian families and friends. I cook Indian food amongst other food and anyone present at the time of dinner shares the food. I try to extend it beyond that—by talking about Indian issues and my views about them, etc.

In October I plan to go to India for a year to spend time working, talking, thinking about what all this means to me and how I can be a part of the changes that are happening in various directions, in particular the question of Indian and other black women.

VIBHA

વિભાવરી   'વાઙ્મયુધ્ધ'

એક ભારતીય વ્યક્તિ હોવાનો અર્થ મારા માટે શો છે? આ એક કઠિન પ્રશ્ન છે જેનો કોઈ સીધો જવાબ મારી પાસે નથી. ભારતીય હોવું એ મારા માટે જીવનની એક હકીકત છે, એક સાંસ્કૃતિક અનુભવ છે છતાં એમાં અંગ્રેજ સંસ્કૃતિનો પ્રભાવ પણ જરૂર છે. છેલ્લા પાંચ વર્ષોથી અંગ્રેજ માણસ સાથે લગ્ન કરીને હું ઈંગ્લેન્ડમાં રહું છું. મારા પતિ જ્યાન સાથે હું પાંચ માસની લાંબી મુલાકાતે ભારત ગઈ હતી. જ્યાન લગ્ન પહેલા પણ ભારતમાં રહેતા હતા. તે સમય દરમિયાન અમારા બંનેની મુલાકાત થઈ હતી. અંગ્રેજ હોવા છતાં તે 'તામિલ' ભાષા બોલી શકે છે. એ ભારતના જીવનની જાણકારીનું એક ઉદાહરણ છે એમની પોતાની સંસ્કૃતિ ઉપરાંત બીજા દેશોની સંસ્કૃતિ વિષેની સમજ એમના માટે ઘણું મહત્ત્વ ધરાવે છે. રાજકીય પરિસ્થિતિ વિષેના વિચારો, સમજ તથા અનુભવો અમારા બંનેના લગભગ સમાન છે.

એક ભારતીય નારી તરીકે મારા અનુભવો જીવન સાથે ઘનિષ્ટ સંબંધ ધરાવે છે. રાજકીય પરિસ્થિતિ વિષેના વિચારો ઘડવામાં અંગ્રેજ અને ઈન્ડિયન બંને સંસ્કૃતિઓનો સુમેળ ઘણું મહત્ત્વ રાખે છે છતાં મારા ભિસ્મો પણ સીમિત છે. મારા માતાપિતાનું ઘર છોડ્યા પછી મેં જે જીવનના અનુભવો મેળવ્યા એની સાથે હું નિષ્ઠાથી સંકળાયેલી છું.

ભારતીય સમાજમાં પિતા વડીલોની સંમતિથી ગોઠવાયેલા લગ્નની પ્રથા, દીકરીને લગ્ન પ્રસંગે માબાપોએ મોઢું દહેજ આપવાની પ્રથા, સમાજમાં રાજા અને રંકના ભેદભાવ, સામાજિક અસમાનતા, શ્રીમંતોના ઘરોમાં નોકરચાકર, બ્યુરોક્રસી તથા દેશી રાજરજવાડાઓની અત્યંત કાર્યવાહી આ બધા પ્રત્યે વિરોધ દર્શાવતા વિચારો મારા મનમાં ઉપસ્થિત થવા લાગ્યા. આ બાબતે મને બીજાઓનો ખૂબ ઓછો સહકાર મળ્યો. મારા મંતવ્યો વિષેનો મારો પોતાનો બચાવ મારે જ કરવાનો હોવાથી હું શાબ્દિક રૂપમાં મારો બચાવ કરતા શીખી. ભારતીય સમાજ વિષેના વિરોધી વિચારોને હું ભારપૂર્વક દર્શાવતા શીખી.

મેં આર્કિટેક્ચર (architecture) નો અભ્યાસ શરૂ કર્યો. પરિણામે હું બે મુખ્ય બાબતો શીખી શકી.

(૧) જે મૂળ પરંપરાઓનો હું વિરોધ કરતી હતી એમાં વધારે ઊંડાણથી હું સંડોવાતી ગઈ. આર્કિટેક્ચર સામાન્ય રીતે સ્ત્રીઓનો પ્રોફેશન ગણાતો નથી. મોટેભાગે શ્રીમંતો અને લાગવગવાળાઓ આ લાઈનમાં જોડાતા હોય છે. આ વિષયનો અભ્યાસ કરતા હું લાગવગ ધરાવતા વધુ પ્રભાવશાળી લોકોના સંઘર્ષમાં આવતી ગઈ. પરિણામે મારા વિરોધી મંતવ્યો હું વધારે ઉગ્ર સ્વરૂપે દર્શાવવા લાગી. મારા નિકટના લોકો જ મારા વિરોધીઓ હોવાથી પરિસ્થિતિ વધારે મુશ્કેલભરી બનતી હતી.

(૨) શાળામાં અભ્યાસ કરતા મેં મારો સમય નકામો જ ગુમાવ્યો હતો. છતાં મારા પોતા વિષે તથા રાજનીતિશાસ્ત્ર વિષે હું ઘણું ઘણું શીખી હતી. કેટલાક આદર્શો અને એને અનુસરીને રહેવાની મારી ઈચ્છાથી જે જૂની રૂઢિઓને કારણે મારો વિકાસ સીમિત બન્યો હતો એ રૂઢિઓને મેં જતી કરી.

મેં પોતે પાકો નિર્ણય કર્યો હતો કે કોઈ મિલકતની જેમ મને લીજ કરીને સુપ્રત કરી દેવાની પ્રથા હું કોઈ પણ સ્વીકારવાની નથી. સાચું કહો તો મારા ઘરમાં હું એક 'પરાયા ધન' એટલે 'પારકાની મિલકત'ની જેમ ઊછરેલી હતી. જ્યારે મારા લગ્નનો પ્રસંગ આવે ત્યારે મારા પિતાજી મારું 'કન્યાદાન' (દિકરીનું દાન) કરે એ બાબતનો હું સખત વિરોધ દર્શાવતી હતી. એને કારણે મારા માતાપિતા સાથે મારે ખૂબ ચર્ચા થતી. ખાસ કરીને મારા પિતા સાથે લાગણીયુક્ત ગરમાગરમ ચર્ચા થતી. ઘણીવાર તેઓની સહાનુભૂતિ મને મળતી પરંતુ ઘણીવાર તેઓ મારા પ્રત્યે કોઈ સહાનુભૂતિ દર્શાવતા નહિ. સમય જતાં ધીરે ધીરે તેઓ મારા વિચારોને સમજવા લાગ્યા.

મારા જીવનના વિકાસ સાથે સાથે મારામાં એક પ્રકારની જણ પેદા થઈ કે આજુબાજુ અન્ય પરિસ્થિતિ પણ છે કે જેને હું આ વિષય સાથે સાંધી શકતી નથી. છતાં એનો આછો ખ્યાલ આપવા હું પ્રયત્ન કરું છું.

ભારતીય મહિલામંડળ આંદોલનમાં ઉપસ્થિત થતા વિચારો કે જે મારા પોતાના કામ સાથે સંબંધ ધરાવે છે એના સંપર્કમાં હું હાલ આવી છું. બ્રિટીશ રાજની સામે ભારતની લડતમાં સ્ત્રીઓનો ફાળો કેવો હતો એ વિષે અભ્યાસ કરવાનું મારું કામ હતું. ઈમ્પીરીયલીઝમનો મેં હંમેશા વિરોધ કર્યો છે અને એના સંઘર્ષમાં હું સતત રહી છું.

બ્રાઇટલિંગસી (Brightling Sea) નામના દરિયાકિનારે વસેલા નાનકડા ગામમાં હું રહું છું. અહિના લોકો પરસ્પર સંપ અને સુમેળ ધરાવે છે. ગામના જે ભાગમાં રહું છું ત્યાં દરેક જણ અડકોઅળાબથી પરિચિત છે. ગામના લોકોએ મને એક ઈન્ડીયન સ્ત્રી તરીકે અપનાવી છે તેથી આ ગામ મને મારા પોતાના ઘર જેવું લાગે છે.

હું એક ભારતની સ્ત્રી છું. ગમે તેવો પોશાક હું પહેરું પરંતુ અમુક અંશે મારામાં એક ભારતીય તત્વ કાયમ રહે છે. મારામાં એવું કંઈક છે જે ભારતનું પ્રતિનિધિત્વ ધરાવે છે. આ બાબતની યોગ્ય પરિભાષા મેળવવા હું પ્રયત્ન કરું છું.

ભારતના અંગ્રેજ રાજનીતિના ઈતિહાસ તથા તેની સામે થયેલ ઈંડીયનોની (ખાસ કરીને મહિલાઓ) જે ઝુંબેશ હતી તે મારા આદર્શો અને વિચારો સાથે નિકટ સંબંધ ધરાવે છે. જીવનમાં દરેક વ્યક્તિને કોઈને કોઈ બાબતે બીજાઓ સાથે સંઘર્ષ થાય છે તેમ મારા વિચારોને લઈને મારે પણ માણસો સાથે સંઘર્ષ થાય છે.

અમારા વિચારો વિરોધી હોવા છતાં અમારી જીંદગી સાથે ઘડાતી જાય છે. અમારા બંનેના પરસ્પરના તથા બીજાઓ સાથેના સંબંધોથી જે સમજ ઉપસ્થિત થાય છે તેનાથી હું બીજા લોકો સાથે સુમેળથી રહી શકું છું.

કદાચ હું જે કહું છું તેમાં કોઈ નાવીન્ય નથી. પણ તે મારા જીવનમાં ઘણું મહત્વ ધરાવે છે. ભારતીય સમાજમાં જેઓ મને ઓળખે છે તેઓ અંગ્રેજોએ પ્રત્યેની તેઓની માન્યતાઓ પ્રમાણે મને જુએ છે. તે જ પ્રમાણે અંગ્રેજ લોકો મને તેઓની ઈન્ડિયન લોકો પ્રત્યેની માન્યતાઓ પ્રમાણે જુએ છે. 'અંગ્રેજ' અને 'ઈન્ડિયન' બંને સંસ્કૃતિઓ જે દર્શાવે છે તેમાંનું જે કાંઈ મારે જતુ કરવાનું છે અને ઘણું મુશ્કેલ (complex) છે. સંસ્કૃતિઓ લોકો વિના ઘડાતી નથી. ઈતિહાસમાં લોકોને 'સંસ્કૃતિ' પર કાબુ ધરાવતો છે પણ તેથી શું ? બીજા સ્ત્રીઓ જેઓ મારી જેમ વિવિધ ક્ષેત્રોમાં સંઘર્ષ ધરાવે છે એમના અનુભવોને મારા અનુભવોથી પર ગણતી નથી. જુદા જુદા રસ્તાઓ અપનાવવામાં ન્યૂઆતો હોય શકે. અમારા અનુભવોનો સુમેળ કરવા અને આ જંગેશનું માણાર્મ્ય દર્શાવવા હું પ્રયત્ન કરું છું. કેટલાંક બાબતો મારે અપનાવવાની છે અને કેટલીક જતી કરવાની છે. આ બાબતે હું પોતાને સંઘર્ષમાં લાવું છું.

ગુજરાતી કુટુંબમાં જે સંયુક્ત કુટુંબની ભાવના છે તેને સમજાવવા હું પ્રયત્ન કરું છું. આ પ્રકારના કુટુંબમાં બિજાોની જરૂરિયાતોને પણ મહત્વ અપાય છે. ભારતીય કુટુંબનું 'ખુલ્લા ઘર'નું વાતાવરણ મને ખૂબ ગમે છે બીજા રસોઈની સાથે સાથે હું ઈન્ડિયન ખોરાક પણ રાંધુ છું. જમવાના સમયે જે કોઈ મારા ઘરમાં હોય છે તે અમારી સાથે ભોજન કરે છે. આ સમયે હું ભારતની સમસ્યાઓ વિશેના મારા વિચારો પણ બિજાો સાથે ચર્ચું છું.

ઑક્ટોબરમાં હું એક વર્ષના ગાળા માટે ઈંડિયા જવાનો પ્લાન કરું છું. આ સમયગાળા દરમિયાન હું ભારતમાં લોકો સાથે કામ કરીશ. વાર્તાલાપો કરીશ અને એ બધાંનું મહત્વ મારા પોતાને માટે શું છે એના વિષે મનન કરીશ. વિવિધ ક્ષેત્રો જેવા કે ઈન્ડિયન અને બીજી કાળી મહિલાઓના વિકાસમાં જે જે ફેરફારો થઈ રહ્યા છે એમાં હું કઈ રીતે મારો ફાળો આપી શકું એ બાબત જાણવા હું પ્રયત્ન કરીશ.

If you enjoyed this book you might like to know about the other books which Centerprise have published.
You can obtain a catalogue by sending a s.a.e. to
The Publishing Project
Centerprise
136/138 Kingsland High St
Hackney
London E8 2NS

There are many other groups involved in similar work around the country. These groups make up the Federation of Worker Writers and Community Publishers which provides a forum for the discussion of issues connected with working class writing and history. It also encourages groups and individuals with their writing and with the wider distribution of their work through its magazine Voices, its annual general meeting and regular visits between its member groups.

Voices
61 Bloom St
Manchester
M1 3LY

FWWCP
Ian Bild, secretary
Bristol Broadsides
100 Cheltenham Rd
Bristol 6